Information
for International Marketing

Information
for International Marketing

An Annotated Guide to Sources

Compiled by
James K. Weekly
and Mary K. Cary

Bibliographies and Indexes in Economics and Economic History, Number 3

GREENWOOD PRESS
New York • Westport, Connecticut • London

LIBRARY OF CONGRESS CATALOGING-IN-PUBLICATION DATA

Weekly, James K., 1933-
   Information for international marketing.

   (Bibliographies and indexes in economics and
economic history, ISSN 0749-1786 ; no. 3)
   Includes index.
   1. Export marketing—Bibliography.   2. Reference
books—Export marketing—Bibliography.   3. Information
storage and retrieval systems—Export marketing—
Bibliography.   4. Export marketing—Information
services—Directories.   I. Cary, Mary K., 1953-
II. Title.   III. Series.
Z7164.C8W4 1986 [HF1009.5] 016.6588'48 86-9954
ISBN 0-313-25440-0 (lib. bdg. : alk. paper)

Library of Congress Catalog Card Number: 86-9954
ISBN: 0-313-25440-0
ISSN: 0749-1786

First published in 1986

Greenwood Press, Inc.
88 Post Road West
Westport, Connecticut 06881

Printed in the United States of America

The paper used in this book complies with the
Permanent Paper Standard issued by the National
Information Standards Organization (Z39.48-1984).

10 9 8 7 6 5 4 3 2 1

Contents

vi   Contents

Preface

The massive expansion of overseas business operations and international trade which has occurred in recent years has created a pressing need for accurate, reliable, and up-to-date information on foreign markets, international business practices, and laws relating to conducting business abroad.

Fortunately, this need has been recognized by a multitude of international institutions, government agencies, and private enterprises. These organizations continuously gather, compile, and disseminate a wealth of data that can be productively used by companies that are engaged in international business or seeking foreign business opportunities.

The problem that many of these companies face is one of locating the best sources of the information which they require. While there is a high probability that virtually any item of information is available, the task of sorting through the vast array of published materials to identify the appropriate source is often a difficult and intimidating one.

The principal aim of this publication is to serve as a guide to the major information sources useful to both the businessperson and the student in international marketing. These sources cover a variety of topics, including economic and political conditions throughout the world, overseas markets, international business techniques, legal rules pertaining to international business operations, companies engaged in foreign production and trade, facilitating organizations, and financial and credit services.

Scope

This guide covers 195 of the most important information sources of particular relevance to those involved in international marketing. It includes references to United States government publications, databases, indexes to periodicals and newspapers, and basic reference sources such as directories, almanacs, encyclopedias, handbooks, and statistical sources. Several relevant loose-leaf publications are also included. The appendixes provide addresses and phone numbers of both private and public agencies that can assist the international marketer. This work is not an exhaustive listing of directories and guidebooks pertaining to specific countries or industries, but rather lists the most essential sources, as well as sources for countries with which United States corporations have extensive business dealings.

The frequency of publication is indicated for those items that are published on a recurring basis. Publication dates are given for items that do not follow a regular publication cycle. Most materials have been published since 1983. Those with older publication dates were considered to be either unique or classic information sources.

Organization

The arrangement of this guide is unique. It is geared not to librarians, as so many source guides are, but to the actual user of international marketing information, the businessperson or student, and is organized by type of information. Each chapter lists useful information sources and includes brief annotations that will help the user in narrowing the search. Many of the information sources contain information useful in several categories. To eliminate the annoying need to flip from one section to another, the full annotation is given each time a source is cited.

Many of the references cited are government publications. The Superintendent of Documents Number, the classification system used to organize these documents in many libraries, is given after the name of the issuing agency. This number can facilitate access to the document in a library collection and ordering from the U.S. Government Printing Office (GPO).

The following sample entry illustrates how to interpret the references:

1   2   3   4

013 **World** **Development** **Report**. Annual. Describes and

analyzes major international economic conditions and

trends. Includes comprehensive and detailed statistics

on population, economic conditions, social conditions,

international trade and investment, and foreign debt for

all IMF and World Bank member countries.

5

The World Bank.

1 Entry number

2 Title of publication

3 Frequency of publication

4 Annotation: Description of contents and type of data

provided

5 Publisher

This guide also lists computer databases useful to the
international marketer and briefly describes database
searching for the "uninitiated."

Several appendixes have been included to further assist
the user. The Directory of Publishers (Appendix A) is a
complete alphabetical list of publishers of the reference
sources cited. It includes addresses and available phone
numbers.

State Trade Contacts (Appendix B) is a comprehensive list
of agencies at the local level that can assist the
international marketer. It includes the U.S. Department of
Commerce offices, state government agencies, port authority
offices, university affiliated centers, and private
agencies.

U.S. Foreign Service Offices in Foreign Countries
(Appendix C) can be used to locate and contact these offices
by mail or telephone. The commercial officers in these
offices continually monitor local economic conditions to
attempt to find market opportunities for U.S. products, and

can be valuable contacts and sources of information for American business firms. Appendix C lists these foreign service offices alphabetically by country and includes the address, phone number, and telex number if available. Some larger foreign countries have several foreign service offices, as well as an export development office.

Foreign Embassies in the United States (Appendix D) can be utilized to locate and contact the official representatives of foreign nations in the United States. These embassies maintain commercial staff personnel who can provide information and assist those interested in exploring or developing business opportunities in their countries. This listing of foreign embassies, all of which are located in Washington, D.C., is arranged alphabetically by country.

The International Trade Administration (ITA) is part of the U.S. Department of Commerce charged with improving trade relations and assisting U.S. companies in marketing overseas. Appendix E provides phone numbers of sections within the ITA concerned with specific products, services, or geographic regions.

Appendix F is a listing of key academic and professional journals in the area of international marketing. It indicates the title of these journals, the frequency of publication, and the name and address of the publisher.

The Title Index at the end of the book provides an alphabetical reference to all sources cited in the book. Those who may know or learn of an information source can refer to this index, note its entry number(s), and then turn to those entries to gain an idea of the source's usefulness by reading its annotation and noting chapter headings.

Availability of Sources

All the sources listed (with the exception of databases) are available for purchase by contacting the publisher directly or through a bookstore. Prices vary from free or inexpensive to over a thousand dollars for an annual subscription. Before deciding to purchase a reference, it would be wise to visit a public or academic library that has an extensive business reference collection. Reviewing the sources firsthand will greatly aid a purchase decision. You may decide that purchase is unnecessary if the library is a convenient place to visit on a regular basis. Ask the librarian if the library is a federal documents depository library. Libraries designated as such receive a variety of sources published by various government agencies that can provide invaluable information related to international marketing. Many of these resources have been identified in this guide, as indicated by the inclusion of the Superintendent of Documents Number (SuDoc #) after the name of the issuing agency.

Acknowledgments

We wish to express our sincere thanks to Lee Jin Lin, Zach Skevofilax, and especially to Gail Stolarski, all of whom helped immeasurably in the preparation of this work. Any omissions or errors are, of course, our own responsibility.

Abbreviations and Acronyms Used in This Guide

Admin.	administration
Assn.	association
Auth.	authority
Bus.	business
Devel.	development
Div.	division
Econ.	economic
EEC	European Economic Community
FAO	Food and Agriculture Organization
FCIA	Foreign Credit Insurance Association
GATT	General Agreement on Tariffs and Trade
GDP	gross domestic product
Hdq.	headquarters
IMF	International Monetary Fund
Intl.	international
ISCO	International Standard Classification of Occupations
ISIC	International Standard Industrial Classification
ITA	International Trade Administration
NTIS	National Technical Information Service
OECD	Organization for Economic Cooperation and Development
Ofc.	office
SuDoc	Superintendent of Documents
UN	United Nations

Information
for International Marketing

I
Demographic Data

001 **Army Area Handbooks**. Irregular. Each handbook in this series discusses a particular foreign country's social institutions, political system, and economic structure. All handbooks include bibliographies providing references to additional sources of information on the country.

United States Army. Su Doc #D 101.22:

002 **Asia Yearbook**. Annual. Includes information on individual countries: finance, investment, economics, trade and aid, organizations, etc.

Far Eastern Economic Review, Ltd.

003 **Demographic Yearbook**. Annual. Comprehensive collection of international demographic statistics. Includes population; demographic and social characteristics; geographical; educational; economic information.

United Nations.

004 **The Economies of the Arabian Gulf**. A statistical source book containing detailed data on population, economic conditions, international trade, governments, labor force, agriculture and land utilization, manufacturing, financial institutions, and education for the Arabian Gulf countries.

Croom Helm, 1984.

005 **The Encyclopedia of the Third World**. 3 Volumes. Provides a compact, balanced and objective description of the dominant political, economic and social systems of 122 countries of the world.

Facts on File, Inc., 1982.

006 **Encyclopedia of the United Nations and International Agreements**. Contains complete text or summaries of major international agreements, explanations of widely used political and economic terms, and organizational details of every United Nations Agency. Also contains world population forecasts and economic data on virtually every country in the world.

Taylor and Francis, Inc., 1985.

007 **Europa Yearbook - A World Survey**. Annual. 2 Volumes.
     Volume 1
     Part I   - International Organizations - activities,
                 address, etc.
     Part II   - Europe
     Part III - Afghanistan - Burundi
     Volume 2
     Cameroon - Zimbabwe
     Includes history, government, economic affairs, etc. of individual countries.

Europa Publications, Limited.

008 **European Marketing Data and Statistics - 1985**. Detailed documentation on the social, economic, and consumer structure of 30 countries in Western and Eastern Europe. Also includes an examination of published data on housing, construction, and the European household.

Euromonitor Publications, Ltd., 1985.
(Distributed by Gale Research Company in the United States).

009 **Rand McNally Commercial Atlas and Marketing Guide**. Annual. Maps of all countries and data on their population, climate, land areas, etc. Includes a descriptive index of each country's political divisions, leading products, exports, imports, and principal ports.

Rand McNally and Company.

010 **Statistical Yearbook.** Annual. Comprehensive compendium of internationally comparable data for the analysis of socio-economic development at the world, regional and national levels.

United Nations.

011 **U.S.S.R. Facts and Figures Annual.** Annual. Includes government, communist party, demography, armed forces, economy, energy, industrial production, industries, agriculture, foreign trade and aid, health, education, welfare, culture and communications, transportation, institutions.

Academic International Press.

012 **World Almanac and Book of Facts.** Annual. Includes data on economic, political and social conditions; arts and media; associations and societies.

Newspaper Enterprise Association, Inc.

013 **World Development Report.** Annual. Describes and analyzes major international economic conditions and trends. Includes comprehensive and detailed statistics on population, economic conditions, social conditions, international trade and investment, and foreign debt for IMF and World Bank member countries.

World Bank.

014 **The World in Figures.** Annual. Detailed figures on each country of the world. Includes population, GNP, area, standard of living, agriculture, education, transportation, manufacturing, mining, energy, etc.

Facts on File, Inc.

015 **Worldwide Economic Indicators: Comparative Summary for 131 Countries.** Annual. Includes key economic indicators; GDP by activity; demographic and labor force data; wages and prices; foreign trade; miscellaneous production and consumption data. Provides basic data to determine comparative market size and to measure the speed at which markets are changing.

Business International Corporation.

016 **Year Book of Labour Statistics**. Annual.   Includes total economically   active   population,   employment, unemployment, hours of work, wages, consumer prices, industrial   accidents,   industrial   disputes.   Also International Standard Industrial Classification and International Standard Classification of Occupations (ISIC and ISCO).

International Labour Organisation
United Nations.

II
Economic Data

017 **American Import/Export Management**. Monthly. Articles
and current news on trade laws and trading
opportunities.

North American Publishing Company.

018 **Annual Report of the International Monetary Fund**.
Annual. Describes major developments in the world
economy and international trade and finance.
Statistical tables on trade, monetary conditions,
national income and product by countries and regions.

International Monetary Fund.

019 **Army Area Handbooks**. Irregular. Each handbook in this
series discusses a particular foreign country's social
institutions, political system, and economic structure.
All handbooks include bibliographies providing
references to additional sources of information on the
country.

United States Army.

020 **Asia Cable**. Monthly. Newsletters providing information
on political, economic, and financial conditions in
Asia.

Asia Cable.

021 **Asia Yearbook**. Annual. Includes information on
individual countries; plus finance, investment,

economics, trade and aid, organizations, etc.

Far Eastern Economic Review, Ltd.

022 **Balance of Payments Statistics**. Annual.
Part I - Alphabetical listing by country - aggregate and
detailed presentations.   Includes current accounts,
direct investments, long-term and short-term capital.
Part II - Data given in Part I is aggregated by category
rather than country.

International Monetary Fund.

023 **Business   America**.   Twice   monthly.   Magazine which
includes current international marketing news and a
regular   listing   of: Licensing   and   investment
opportunities abroad; exporting opportunities; foreign
firms   interested   in   agency   or   distributorship
arrangements with U.S. firms; foreign construction
projects.

U.S. Department of Commerce. Su Doc #C61.18:

024 **Business Asia**. Weekly. Newsletter which offers short
articles on economy, banking, management, licensing,
etc. for Asian regions.

Business International Corporation

025 **Business Eastern Europe**. Weekly. Newsletter which
offers short articles on economy, banking, management,
licensing, etc. for Eastern European regions.

Business International Corporation.

026 **Business Environment Risk Information**. Tri-annual.
Assessments of political risks, economic trends,
currency convertibility, business operating conditions,
and profit opportunities for each of 48 countries.

IRM (International Research and Marketing), Inc.

027 **Business Europe**. Weekly. Newsletter which offers short
articles on economy, interest rates, investment,
marketing, personnel, currency, management, etc. for
European regions.

Business International Corporation.

028 **Business   International**.   Weekly.   Newsletter   which offers   short   articles   on   capital   sources,   codes   of conduct,   currency,   economy,   exporting,   foreign   trade, management,   marketing.

Business International Corporation.

029 **Business   International   Money   Report**.   Weekly. Newsletter   which   offers   short   articles   on   accounting, capital   sources,   stock   and   bond   financing,   eurobonds, currency,   financial   techniques,   etc.

Business International Corporation.

030 **Business   International   Research   Reports**.   Irregular. In-depth   studies   of   particular   foreign   countries   or regions,   important   developments   affecting   international business,   and   international   business   problems.

Business International Corporation.

031 **Business   Latin   America**.   Weekly.   Newsletter   which offers   short   articles   on   commodities,   economy,   industry, personnel   and   labor,   importing,   investment,   etc.   for Latin   American   regions.

Business International Corporation.

032 **Commodity   Year   Book**.   Annual.   Designed   to   aid   in   the appraisal   of   commodity   price   prospects   -   domestic   and international.

Commodity Research Bureau, Inc.

033 **Direction   of   Trade   Statistics**.   Annual.   Data   on   the distribution   by   trade   partners   of   total   exports   and imports   for   154   countries,   as   well   as   area   and   world aggregates   showing   trade   flows   among   major   areas   of   the world.

International Monetary Fund.

034 **The   Dow   Jones-Irwin   Business   and   Investment   Almanac**. Annual.   Includes   business   in   review   (daily   basis); breakdown   of   industries   -   textiles,   metals,   energy; financial   statements   by   industry;   stock   market,

commodities markets.   Includes some international.

Dow Jones-Irwin.

035 **Economic Forecasts: A Worldwide Survey**.   Monthly.   A
    journal which presents and discusses forecasts of real
    GNP, inflation, unemployment, interest rates, and other
    major   economic   variables   for   the   principal
    industrialized and trading countries.

    Elsevier Science Publishers.

036 **The Economies of the Arabian Gulf**. A statistical source
    book containing detailed data on population, economic
    conditions,   international   trade,   governments,   labor
    force, agriculture and land utilization, manufacturing,
    financial institutions, and education for the Arabian
    Gulf countries.

    Croom Helm, 1984.

037 **The Encyclopedia of the Third World**.   3 Volumes.
    Provides a compact, balanced and objective description
    of the dominant political, economic and social systems
    of 122 countries of the world.

    Facts on File, Inc., 1982.

038 **Encyclopedia of the United Nations and International
    Agreements**.   Contains complete text or summaries of
    major international agreements, explanations of widely
    used political and economic terms, and organizational
    details of every United Nations Agency.   Also contains
    world   population   forecasts   and   economic   data   on
    virtually every country in the world.

    Taylor and Francis, Inc., 1985.

039 **Europa Yearbook - A World Survey**.   Annual.   2 Volumes.
       Volume 1
    Part I - International Organizations - activities,
       address, etc.
    Part II - Europe
    Part III - Afghanistan - Burundi
       Volume 2
    Cameroon - Zimbabwe

Includes history, government, economic affairs, etc. of individual countries.

Europa Publications, Limited.

040 **European Marketing Data and Statistics - 1985.** Detailed documentation on the social, economic, and consumer structure of 30 countries in Western and Eastern Europe. Also includes an examination of published data on housing, construction, and the European household.

Euromonitor Publications, Ltd., 1985.
(Distributed by Gale Research Company in the United States).

041 **Export.** Bimonthly. Information on foreign markets for exporters of durable goods.

Johnson International Publishing Company.

042 **FAO Trade Yearbook.** Annual. Statistical data on trade in agricultural products and value of agricultural trade, by countries.

Food and Agriculture Organization.
United Nations.

043 **Foreign Economic Trends.** Irregular. Country-by-country reviews of current business conditions, latest data on GNP, foreign trade, wage and price indexes, unemployment rates, and construction starts.

U.S. Department of Commerce. Su Doc #C42.30:

044 **Foreign Exchange Yearbook.** Annual. A listing of daily foreign exchange and Eurocurrency deposit rates for leading world currencies with a commentary on international developments.

Woodhead-Faulkner, Limited.

045 **F & S Index Europe.** Annual. Indexes current articles on European companies and industries. Arranged in 3 sections:
Section 1 - Industries and products - arranged by SIC
Section 2 - Entries arranged by region
Section 3 - Companies - alphabetical

Predicasts, Inc.

046 **F & S International**. Annual. Indexes current articles
on foreign companies and industries. Arranged in three
sections:
Section 1 - industries and products
Section 2 - countries
Section 3 - companies

Predicasts, Inc.

047 **Guide to World Commodity Markets**. Commodity market data
on various areas of the world.

Kogan Page, Limited, 4th Edition, 1985.

048 **Handbook of Economic Statistics**. Contains economic
profiles and trends for all communist countries and
selected non-communist countries. Statistical data on
foreign trade and aid, energy, manufacturing, minerals
and metals, agriculture, transportation, and forestry.

U.S. Central Intelligence Agency, 1983. Su Doc #PrEx3
10/7:

049 **Handbook of National Development Plans**. Supplemental
updates issued semi-annually. Summarizes the economic
development plans of over seventy countries. Includes
background economic data on each country.

Metra Consulting, Graham and Trotman.

050 **IMF Survey**. Twice monthly. Digest of news on
international trade, finance, and economic developments,
as well as economic conditions and events within
particular countries.

International Monetary Fund.

051 **International Bibliography, Information, Documentation**.
Quarterly. Subject Classifications: commerce and
business, culture, international economic relations,
international law, international organization,
international relations, etc.

Unipub (A Xerox Publishing Company).

052 **International   Economic   Indicators.**   Quarterly.
Comparative economic statistics for U.S. and seven major
foreign countries.

U.S. Department of Commerce. Su Doc #C61.14:

053 **International   Finance   Handbook.**   2   Volumes.
Comprehensive handbook on international finance. Gives
practical   guidance   on   foreign   exchange   management,
international money and capital markets, international
financing techniques and sources.

John Wiley and Sons, Inc., 1983.

054 **International** **Financial** **Statistics**. Monthly. Data on
exchange   rates,   international   reserves,   money   and
banking,   international   trade,   prices,   production,
interest   rates,   and   government   finance   for   all
International Monetary Fund member countries.

International Monetary Fund.

055 **International** **Marketing** **Data** **and** **Statistics**. Reference
work   provides   variety   of   statistical   data   on   132
countries: Statistical   data   measuring   over   100   key
factors concerning population, production, and trade,
marketing   and   demographic   data   presented   on   132
countries throughout the world.

Gale Research Company, 9th Edition, 1985.

056 **International** **Marketing** **Handbook**.   2 Volumes.   Includes
a marketing profile for every nation in the Western
world   which   offers   a   substantial   export   market,   and
gives an in-depth market analysis for countries with
which American firms deal most commonly.   Also includes
fundamental trade data for Eastern Bloc countries, plus
Near East and North African countries.

Gale Research Company, 1983.

057 **International** **Reports** **Weekly**.   Weekly.   Newsletters
covering upcoming developments in 100 countries around
the world - foreign exchange - bond and loan markets.

International Reports, Inc.

058 **International Trade**. Annual. Detailed report on worldwide economic output and international trade.

General Agreement on Tariffs and Trade (GATT).

059 **International Trade Reporter**. Regularly up-dated. Country-by-country surveys of international trade situation, trade and exchange controls, and methods of handling export shipments.

Bureau of National Affairs, Inc.

060 **Investing, Licensing and Trading Conditions Abroad**. Regularly updated. Detailed information on state role in industry; rules of competition; price controls; licensing; remittability of funds; corporate taxes; personal taxes; incentives; capital sources; labor; foreign trade. Covers all countries or regions of the world.

Business International Corporation.

061 **Journal of Commerce**. Daily. Current information on international economic developments and foreign trade. Includes extensive shipping information and ship schedules.

Twin Coast Newspapers, Inc.

062 **Marketing Europe 1985**. 2 Volumes.
Volume I. Provides country-by-country coverage of political and economic conditions, plus statistics pertaining to retailing, advertising, and media. Includes a marketer's directory with names and addresses of key advertising agencies, media, retailers, and research firms, as well as sources of marketing data.
Volume II. Treats sixteen European countries as a single market entity and describes major trends and developments in that market.

Adweek.

063 **National Accounts of OECD Countries**.
Vol. I: 1951-1980
Vol. II: 1963-1980
Vol. I: Gives for each country the main aggregates calculated according to either the present or former Systems of National Accounts. Graphs, comparative tables, purchasing power parities.
Vol. II: Detailed statistics - main aggregates, gross domestic product, government final consumption

expenditure; distribution of national disposable income.

Organization for Economic Cooperation and Development, 1982.

064 **National Accounts Statistics**. Annual. 3 Volumes.
Volume I: Main Agregates and Detailed Tables.
Volume II: Analysis of Main Aggregates.
Volume III: Government Accounts and Tables.
Provides   comprehensive   national   accounts   data,
summarizes   main   national   account   aggregates   in
analytical   tables,   and   gives   detailed   data   on   the
government sector for 159 countries.

United Nations.

065 **OECD Economic Outlook**. Twice yearly. Reviews recent
economic developments in the OECD area and forecasts
economic conditions in OECD countries for upcoming
twelve month period.

Organization for Economic Cooperation and Development.

066 **OECD Economic Surveys**. Annual. Economic surveys of
each of the 24 OECD member countries, containing
information on current trends in demand and output,
prices and wages, foreign trade and payments, economic
policies, and future economic prospects.

Organization for Economic Cooperation and Development.

067 **Overseas Business Reports**. Irregular. Each report
covers one country and provides information on the
economy, foreign trade regulations, requirements for
establishing a business, marketing channels, etc.

U.S. Department of Commerce.

068 **Pick's Currency Yearbook**. Annual. Offers a complete
review of exchange rate and currency developments
throughout the world, including restrictions, black
market position, etc. Also a description of prices and
movements of gold in international trading centers.

Pick Publishing Corporation.

069 **Polk's World Bank Directory: International Section.**
Semiannual. Alphabetical index to banks - indexed
according to continent, then country. Lists address,
officers, current statement, correspondents.

R.L. Polk and Company, 1982.

070 **Price   Waterhouse   Guide   Series: Doing   Business   in
(Foreign   Countries).**   Revised   regularly.   Detailed
information   on   company   laws,   business   conditions,
taxation in specific foreign countries.

Price Waterhouse and Company.

071 **Rand McNally Commercial Atlas and Marketing Guide.**
Annual.   Maps of all countries and data on their
population, climate, land areas, etc.   Includes a
descriptive index of each country's political divisions,
leading products, exports, imports, and principal ports.

Rand McNally and Company.

072 **Rand McNally International Bankers Directory.** Updated
regularly.   U.S. and international bank listings -
address, statement of condition, correspondents, cable
number, chair; manager, etc.

Rand McNally and Company.

073 **Rundt's Weekly Intelligence.** Weekly. Current, country-
by-country assessments of economic conditions and trade
opportunities.

S.J. Rundt Associates.

074 **Statistical Yearbook.** Annual. Comprehensive compendium
of internationally comparable data for the analysis of
socio-economic development at the world, regional and
national levels.

United Nations.

075 **Statistics of Foreign Trade, Series A, B, and C.**
Annual. Detailed export and import statistics for OECD
member countries.

Organization for Economic Cooperation and Development.

076 **Third World Economic Handbook**.   Extensive economic data
on Third World countries.

Gale Research Company, 1982.

077 **U.S. Export Weekly**.   Weekly.   Current   developments
affecting U.S. exports, including trade legislation,
foreign exchange, financing activities and arrangements,
and economic conditions.

Bureau of National Affairs, Inc.

078 **U.S.S.R. Facts and Figures Annual**.   Annual.   Includes
government, commmunist party, demography, armed forces,
economy, energy, industrial production, industries,
agriculture, foreign trade and aid, health, education,
welfare, culture and communications, transportation,
institutions.

Academic International Press.

079 **World Almanac and Book of Facts**.   Annual.   Includes data
on economic, political and social conditions; arts and
media; associations and societies.

Newspaper Enterprise Association, Inc.

080 **World Development Report**.   Annual.   Describes   and
analyzes major international economic conditions and
trends.   Includes comprehensive and detailed statistics
on population, economic conditions, social conditions,
international trade and investment, and foreign debt for
IMF and World Bank member countries.

World Bank.

081 **World Economic Outlook**.   Annual.   Provides   a
comprehensive picture of the economic situation and
prospects for the world as a whole and for major world
regions.   Analyses of inflation, rates of interest,
exchange rates, trade balances, commodity prices, and
indebtedness are included.

International Monetary Fund.

082 **The World in Figures**. Annual. Detailed figures on each country of the world. Includes population, GNP, area, standard of living, agriculture, education, transportation, manufacturing, mining, energy, etc.

Facts on File, Inc.

083 **World Political Risk Forecasts**. Monthly. Economic data and assessments of political risk for 70 countries.

Frost and Sullivan, Inc.

084 **World Sources of Marketing Information**.
Volume I.   Asia/Pacific
Volume II.   Africa/Middle East
Volume III. Europe
General economic information, censuses of manufacturing and distribution, and detailed marketing research reports covering the major countries of each region.

Ballinger Publishing Company, 1982.

085 **World Tables: The Third Edition (1984)**. An update of economic, demographic and social data relating to practically all countries in the world. Presents time series for a number of basic economic variables for each country.

Published for the World Bank by
The Johns Hopkins University Press.

086 **World Trade News**. Monthly. Analysis of topics of current interest relating to international trade and brief reports on foreign countries and regions.

World Trade Education Center, Cleveland State University.

087 **Worldwide Economic Indicators**. Annual. Includes key economic indicators; GDP by activity; demographic and labor force data; wages and prices; foreign trade; miscellaneous production and consumption data. Provides basic data to determine comparative market size and to measure the speed at which markets are changing.

Business International Corporation, 1983.

088 **Year Book of Labour Statistics**. Annual. Includes total and economically active population, employment, unemployment, hours of work, wages, consumer prices,

industrial   accidents,   industrial   disputes.   Also
International   Standard   Industrial   Classification;
International   Standard   Classification   of   Occupations
(ISIC and ISCO).

International Labour Organisation
United Nations.

089 **Yearbook** **of** **International** **Trade** **Statistics**.   Annual.
Provides the basic information for individual countries'
external trade performances in terms of overall trends
in current value as well as in volume and price, the
importance of trading partners and the significance of
individual commodities imported and exported.
Vol. I - alphabetical by country.
Vol. II - by commodity.

United Nations.

III
Market Data

090 **American Export Marketer**. Monthly. Current information on export support services, taxes and export controls, exchange rates, product marketing opportunities, and economic and political developments affecting exporting.

The American Export Marketer.

091 **Annual Worldwide Industry Review (AWIR)**. Annual. A multi-country "view for the year" which focuses on a particular U.S. industry's export prospects in a number of selected countries. Each report includes 3 parts: U.S. export trends, market assessment, and statistical tables showing U.S. exports of the industry's products to each country.

U.S. Department of Commerce.

092 **Bottin International**. Annual. Names and addresses of manufacturers, exporters, and service firms throughout the world. Classified by country and by products. International business register.

Societe Didot-Bottin (Paris).

093 **Business America**. Twice monthly. Magazine which includes current international marketing news and a regular listing of: Licensing and investment opportunities abroad; exporting opportunities; foreign firms interested in agency or distributorship arrangements with U.S. firms; foreign construction projects.

U.S. Department of Commerce.

094 **Consumer Markets Series**.   Revised regularly.   Series
includes:
    Consumer Markets in the Middle East
    Consumer Markets in North Africa
    Consumer Markets in West Africa
    Consumer Markets in Latin America
    Consumer Markets in Central America
    Consumer Markets in the Far East
    Consumer Markets in the Indian Sub-Continent

This series of volumes focuses upon developing markets
around the world.   Provides statistics on key market
factors and includes regional overviews, inter-country
comparisons, and in-depth country profiles.

Euromonitor Publications.
(Distributed by Gale Research Company in the United
States).

095 **Country Market Sectoral Surveys**.   Irregular.   Reviews by
industry and product category to identify the 10 to 15
"most marketable" products in individual foreign
countries.

U.S. Department of Commerce.   Su Doc #C57.119:

096 **European Marketing Data and Statistics - 1985**.   Detailed
documentation on the social, economic, and consumer
structure of 30 countries in Western and Eastern Europe.
Also includes an examination of published data on
housing, construction, and the European household.

Euromonitor Publications, Ltd., 1985.
(Distributed by Gale Research Company in the United
States).

097 **Export**.   Bimonthly.   Information on foreign markets for
exporters of durable goods.

Johnson International Publishing Company.

098 **Export Briefs**.   Weekly.   Trade leads for agricultural
products.

U.S. Department of Agriculture.   Su Doc #A67.40/2:

099 **Export Promotion Calendar**. Quarterly. Lists U.S. trade promotion events held abroad. Indexed by product, giving data and location of each event.

U.S. Department of Commerce, International Trade Administration. Su Doc #C61.19:

100 **FAO Trade Yearbook**. Annual. Statistical data on trade in agricultural products and value of agricultural trade, by countries.

Food and Agriculture Organization.
United Nations.

101 **Market Share Reports**. Irregular. Statistical reports on trade in manufactured products, showing U.S. shares in markets of foreign countries.

U.S. Department of Commerce. (For sale by National Technical Information Service - NTIS).

102 **Overseas Business Reports**. Irregular. Each report covers one country and provides information on the economy, foreign trade regulations, requirements for establishing a business, marketing channels, etc.

U.S. Department of Commerce.

103 **Rundt's Weekly Intelligence**. Weekly. Current, country-by-country assessments of economic conditions and trade opportunities.

S.J. Rundt Associates.

104 **Statistics of Foreign Trade, Series A, B, and C.** Annual. Detailed export and import statistics for OECD member countries.

Organization for Economic Cooperation and Development.

105 **TOP Bulletin**. Weekly. Up-to-date and detailed listing of foreign market and trade opportunities for U.S. companies on a product-by-product basis.

U.S. Department of Commerce.

106 **Trade Lists**. Names and addresses of foreign companies that are interested in handling particular U.S. products or commodities. Also regional lists of importers,

distributors and agents for certain product groupings.

U.S. Department of Commerce.

107 **U.S. Exports - Commodity by Country** (Bureau of the
Census, FT-410). Monthly. Cumulative data on U.S.
exports, classified by commodity and country of
destination.

U.S. Department of Commerce. Su Doc #C3.164:

108 **U.S. Imports - Commodity by Country** (Bureau of the
Census, FT-135). Monthly. Cumulative data on U.S.
imports, classified by commodity and country of origin.

U.S. Department of Commerce.

109 **World Sources of Market Information.**
   Volume I. Asia/Pacific
   Volume II. Africa/Middle East
   Volume III. Europe
General economic information, censuses of manufacturing
and distribution, and detailed marketing research
reports covering the major countries of each region.

Ballinger Publishing Company, 1982.

110 **World Trade News.** Monthly. Analysis of topics of
current interest relating to international trade and
brief reports on foreign countries and regions.

World Trade Education Center, Cleveland State
University.

111 **Worldwide Economic Indicators.** Annual. Includes key
economic indicators; GDP by activity; demographic and
labor force data; wages and prices; foreign trade;
miscellaneous production and consumption data. Provides
basic data to determine comparative market size and to
measure the speed at which markets are changing.

Business International Corporation.

112 **Yearbook of International Trade Statistics.** Annual.
Provides the basic information for individual countries'
external trade performances in terms of overall trends
in current value as well as in volume and price, the
importance of trading partners and the significance of
individual commodities imported and exported.

24   Market Data

Vol. I - alphabetical by country.
Vol. II - by commodity.

United Nations.

IV
Legal Data

113 **American Export Marketer**. Monthly. Current information on export support services, taxes and export controls, exchange rates, product marketing opportunities, and economic and political developments affecting exporting.

The American Export Marketer.

114 **American Import/Export Management**. Monthly. Articles and current news on trade laws and trading opportunities.

North American Publishing Company.

115 **Annual Report on Exchange Arrangements and Exchange Restrictions**. Annual. Country-by-country review of foreign exchange controls and trade restrictions for all International Monetary Fund member countries.

International Monetary Fund.

116 **Antitrust and Trade Policies of the European Economic Community**. Updated annually. Examination of competition and trade issues of EEC laws includes state aids, antidumping and countervailing duties, commission procedures and actions on competition proceedings, abuse of a dominant position, and many more competition and trade problems in EEC laws.

Matthew Bender and Co., Inc.

117 **Business America**. Twice monthly. Magazine which
includes current international marketing news and a
regular listing of: Licensing and investment
opportunities abroad; exporting opportunities; foreign
firms interested in agency or distributorship
arrangements with U.S. firms; foreign construction
projects.

U.S. Department of Commerce.

118 **Business Asia**. Weekly. Newsletter which offers short
articles on economy, banking, management, licensing,
etc. for Asian regions.

Business International Corporation.

119 **Business Eastern Europe**. Weekly. Newsletter which
offers short articles on economy, banking, management,
licensing, etc. for Eastern European regions.

Business International Corporation.

120 **Business Europe**. Weekly. Newsletter which offers short
articles on economy, interest rates, investment,
marketing, personnel, currency, management etc. for
European regions.

Business International Corporation.

121 **Business International**. Weekly. Newsletter which
offers short articles on capital sources, codes of
conduct, currency, economy, exporting, foreign trade,
management, marketing.

Business International Corporation.

122 **Business Latin America**. Weekly. Newsletter which
offers short articles on commodities, economy, industry,
personnel and labor, importing, investment, etc. for
Latin American regions.

Business International Corporation.

123 **The Chase World Guide for Exporters**. Contains import
and foreign exchange regulations for more than 100
countries.

The World Information Corporation (Chase Manhattan
Bank), 1985.

124 **Commercial, Business and Trade Laws.** Continuously
updated. Series covering different countries and
regions of the world, summarizes laws and regulations
relating to business and trade. Issued country by
country.

Oceana Publications, Inc.

125 **The Encyclopedia of the Third World.** 3 Volumes.
Provides a compact, balanced and objective description
of the dominant political, economic and social systems
of 122 countries of the world.

Facts on File, Inc., 1982.

126 **Export Administration Regulations.** Regularly updated.
Compilation of official U.S. export regulations and
policies governing the exporting and licensing of
products and technical data. Includes Commodity Control
List of products subject to export controls and those
requiring validated licenses.

U.S. Department of Commerce.

127 **Export Documentation Handbook.** Annual with updates.
Gives specific details of documentation requirements for
each country.

Dun's Marketing Services (Dun and Bradstreet
International).

128 **Export Shipping Manual (International Trade Reporter).**
Updated when necessary. Export shipping guide giving
country-by-country import regulations and documentary
requirements.

Bureau of National Affairs, Inc.

129 **Exporter's Encyclopedia.** Annual. Provides the
following data on a country by country basis:
   Section I - The Export Order
   Section II - Export Markets - regulations,
      documentation, business travel
   Section III - Export Know-How
   Section IV - Communications
   Section V - Information Sources/Services
   Section VI - Transportation Data/Services

Dun and Bradstreet International.

130 **Forex Service**. Monthly. A newsletter describing current legal developments affecting international finance and trade. Highlights changes in trade, foreign exchange, and tax regulations.

International Reports, Inc.

131 **International Bibliography, Information, Documentation**. Quarterly. Subject Classifications: commerce and business, culture, international economic relations, international law, international organization, international relations, etc.

Unipub (A Xerox Publishing Company).

132 **International Trade Reporter**. Regularly updated. Country-by-country surveys of international trade situation, trade and exchange controls, and methods of handling export shipments.

Bureau of National Affairs, Inc.

133 **Investing, Licensing and Trading Conditions Abroad**. Regularly updated. Detailed information on state role in industry; rules of competition; price controls; licensing; remittability of funds; corporate taxes; personal taxes; incentives; capital sources; labor; foreign trade. Covers all countries or regions of the world.

Business International Corporation.

134 **OECD Economic Surveys**. Annual. Economic surveys of each of the 24 OECD member countries, containing information on current trends in demand and output, prices and wages, foreign trade and payments, economic policies, and future economic prospects.

Organization for Economic Cooperation and Development.

135 **Overseas Business Reports**. Irregular. Each report covers one country and provides information on the economy, foreign trade regulations, requirements for establishing a business, marketing channels, etc.

U.S. Department of Commerce.

136 **Pick's Currency Yearbook**. Annual. Offers a complete review of exchange rate and currency developments throughout the world, including restrictions, black market position, etc. Also a description of prices and movements of gold in international trading centers.

Pick Publishing Corporation.

137 **Price Waterhouse Guide Series**: **Doing Business in (foreign countries)**. Irregular. Detailed information on company laws, business conditions, taxation in specific foreign countries.

Price Waterhouse and Company.

138 **Reference Book for World Traders**. Monthly. Information needed to execute export and import transactions with all foreign countries. Lists trade organizations, credit information agencies, banks, customs brokers, advertising agencies, and attorneys, as well as export documentation requirements.

Croner Publications.

139 **Strategic Trade Controls Report**. Weekly. Newsletters on national security and foreign policy trade restrictions. Information on the activities of the Department of Commerce's Office of Export Enforcement, Treasury's Customs Service, the State Department and other federal agencies.

Capital Publications, Inc.

140 **U.S. Customs and International Trade Guide**. 4 Volumes. Semiannual. Analysis of the laws, rules, regulations and procedures involved in importing goods to the U.S.A. as well as the latest developments in international trade. Includes customs regulations and tariff schedules, customs exemptions and preferences.

Matthew Bender and Co., Inc.

141 **U.S. Export Weekly**. Weekly. Current developments affecting U.S. exports, including trade legislation, foreign exchange, financing activities and arrangements, and economic conditions.

Bureau of National Affairs, Inc.

142 **United States International Trade Reports**. Continuously updated. Decisions of the U.S. Court of International Trade and the Court of Customs and Patent Appeals.

Oceana Publications, Inc.

143 **World Tax Series**. Irregular. Each volume gives extensive tax data for the country covered, including the tax laws and structure. Also provides detailed analyses of the income tax, tax treatment of foreign income, sales, export and mining levies.

Commerce Clearing House, Inc., in cooperation with the Harvard Law School's International Tax Program.

V
Company Data

144 **American Export Register**. Annual. Comprehensive directory of American manufacturers selling to world markets.

Thomas International Publishing.

145 **Asia Yearbook**. Annual. Includes information on individual countries: finance, investment, economics, trade and aid, organizations, etc.

Far Eastern Economic Review, Ltd.

146 **Bottin International**. Annual. Names and addresses of manufacturers, exporters, and service firms throughout the world. Classified by country and by products. International business register.

Societe Didot-Bottin (Paris).

147 **Business America**. Twice monthly. Magazine which includes current international marketing news and a regular listing of: Licensing and investment opportunities abroad; exporting opportunities; foreign firms interested in agency or distributorship arrangements with U.S. firms; foreign construction projects.

U.S. Department of Commerce.

148 **Directory of Foreign Firms Operating in the U.S.**
1. Alphabetical listing by country - shows American

company and parent company.
2.   Alphabetical listing of foreign parent companies and corresponding American subsidiaries or affiliates.
3.   Alphabetical listing of American subsidiaries, branches or affiliates of foreign companies.

World Trade Academy Press, Inc., 5th Edition, 1983.

149 **Europe's 15,000 Largest Companies** Lists and ranks the largest industrial companies in Europe. Also lists Europe's largest trading companies, transport companies, banks, insurance companies, and advertising agencies.

Dun and Bradstreet International, 1985.

150 **F & S Index Europe**.   Annual.   Indexes current articles on European companies and industries.   Arranged in 3 sections:
Section 1 - Industries and products - arranged by SIC
Section 2 - Entries arranged by region
Section 3 - Companies - alphabetical

Predicasts, Inc.

151 **F & S International**.   Annual.   Indexes current articles on foreign companies and industries.   Arranged in three sections:
Section 1 - industries and products
Section 2 - countries
Section 3 - companies

Predicasts, Inc.

152 **GreenBook - International Directory of Marketing Research Houses and Services**.   Annual.   Listing of market research firms - includes name, address, phone number, principal executives, type of services offered. Alphabetical listing, then late listings and geographic/telephone listings; personnel index and computer programs listing.

New York Chapter of the American Marketing Association.

153 **Kelly's Manufacturer's and Merchants Directory 1981-82**.
Section 1 - Classified - details of manufacturers, merchants, wholesalers and firms offering an industrial service.
Section 2 - Company Information Section - all companies in classified section are listed alphabetically with

trade description, address and communication details. Section 3 - International Exporters and Services - details of companies who export goods worldwide.

Kelly's Directories, Ltd., 1982.

154 **Major Companies of the Far East, 1985**. 2 Volumes. Brief information on major business firms operating in Southeast and East Asia.

Graham and Trotman, Limited, 1985.

155 **Marketing Europe 1985**. 2 Volumes.
Volume I. Provides country-by-country coverage of political and economic conditions, plus statistics pertaining to retailing, advertising, and media. Includes a marketer's directory with names and addresses of key advertising agencies, media, retailers, and research firms, as well as sources of marketing data.
Volume II. Treats sixteen European countries as a single market entity and describes major trends and developments in that market.

Adweek.

156 **Moody's Industrial Manual**. Annual. Alphabetical index to companies. Financial information includes 7-year presentation of income accounts, balance sheets, financial and operation ratios; detailed description of business; capital structure, etc.

Moody's Investors Service, Inc.

157 **Moody's International Manual**. Annual. Financial information on international companies by country of operation.

Moody's Investors Service, Inc.

158 **Principal International Businesses: The World Marketing Directory**. Annual. Directory of major international companies, arranged in 3 sections:
Section 1 - Businesses categorized by geographic location (alphabetized by country)
Section 2 - Businesses categorized by product classification
Section 3 - Businesses listed alphabetically

Dun and Bradstreet International.

159 **Statistics   -   Africa**.   Irregular.   Describes organizations and publications providing statistical information for economic, social and market research for all countries of Africa.

CBD Research, Ltd.

160 **Statistics   -   America**.   Irregular.   Describes organizations and publications providing statistical information for economic, social and market research in North, Central and South America.

CBD Research, Ltd.

161 **Statistics - Asia and Australasia**. Irregular. Describes organizations and publications providing statistical information for economic, social and market research for all countries in Asia, Australasia and Oceania.

CBD Research, Ltd.

162 **Statistics   -   Europe**.   Irregular.   Describes organizations and publications providing statistical information for economic, social and market research in Western and Eastern Europe.

CBD Research, Ltd.

163 **Trade Lists**. Irregular. Names and addresses of foreign companies that are interested in handling particular U.S. products of commodities. Also regional lists of importers, distributors, and agents for certain product groupings.

U.S. Department of Commerce.

164 **World Almanac and Book of Facts**. Annual. Includes data on economic, political and social conditions; arts and media; associations and societies.

Newspaper Enterprise Association, Inc.

165 **World Traders Data Reports**. Irregular. Descriptive, financial, and credit data on individual foreign firms.

U.S. Department of Commerce.

166 **World-Wide Chamber of Commerce Directory**. Annual. Listing of U.S. Chambers of Commerce; American Chambers of Commerce abroad and chief executive officers; Canadian Chambers of Commerce and regional offices; Foreign Chambers of Commerce in principal cities of the world; Dean of diplomatic corps; Foreign embassies and consulates in U.S.; U.S. consulates and embassies in the world; Foreign consular offices in U.S.; manager or president of Chambers of Commerce.

Johnson International Publishing Company, Inc.

VI
Methodological Data

167 **American Export Marketer**. Monthly. Current information
on export support services, taxes and export controls,
exchange rates, product market opportunities, and
economic and political developments affecting exporting.

The American Export Marketer.

168 **Business Asia**. Weekly. Newsletter which offers short
articles on economy, banking, management, licensing,
etc. for Asian regions.

Business International Corporation.

169 **Business Eastern Europe**. Weekly. Newsletter which
offers short articles on economy, banking, management,
licensing, etc. for Eastern European regions.

Business International Corporation.

170 **Business Europe**. Weekly. Newsletter which offers short
articles on economy, interest rates, investment,
marketing, personnel, currency, management etc. for
European regions.

Business International Corporation.

171 **Business International**. Weekly. Newsletter which
offers short articles on capital sources, codes of
conduct, currency, economy, exporting, foreign trade,
management, marketing.

Business International Corporation.

172 **Business International Management Monographs**. Analyses and recommendations centering upon specific problems in international business operations and international management.

Business International Corporation.

173 **Business Latin America**. Weekly. Newsletter which offers short articles on commodities, economy, industry, personnel and labor, importing, investment, etc. for Latin American regions.

Business International Corporation.

174 **Countertrade: Business Practices for Today's World Market**. This book offers thorough definitions and descriptions of various countertrade practices in current use, as well as specific guidelines for negotiating and drafting countertrade contracts. Also includes a country-by-country guide to countertrade opportunities in the Eastern Bloc countries.

American Management Association, 1982.

175 **Documentary Credits: 1974 Rules and 1983 Rules Compared and Explained**. Explains the changes in the 1983 revision of the uniform customs and practices applicable to documents used in extending credit in international trade and the reasons for those changes.

International Chamber of Commerce, 1984.

176 **Documentary Credits: Uniform Customs and Practices for Documentary Credits**. Complete official text of the 1983 revision of the uniform customs and practices applicable to letters of credit and other documents used in extending credit in international trade.

International Chamber of Commerce, 1983 Revision.

177 **Dynamics of Trade Finance**. Overview of the workings of international trade and finance. Topics include: Mechanics of trade financing, documentary collections, commercial letter of credit, bank undertakings, export factoring, foreign exchange, etc.

The Chase Manhattan Bank, 1984.

178 **Export Advisory Reference Manual**. Annual. A handbook containing information on export credit and collections, documentation, import/export regulations, government financing and insurance programs.

Chemical Bank - Export Advisory Service.

179 **Export Documentation Handbook**. Annual with updates. Gives specific details of documentation requirements for each country.

Dun's Marketing Services (Dun and Bradstreet International).

180 **Export Financing: A Handbook of Sources and Techniques**. A handbook detailing new ways of financing exports using less traditional sources and techniques and revealing the less obvious risks and benefits.

Financial Executives Research Foundation (FERF).

181 **Export Shipping Manual**. Continuously updated. Detailed information of U.S. export controls and import regulations applicable to all foreign countries.

Bureau of National Affairs, Inc.

182 **Exporter's Encyclopedia**. Annual. Provides the following data on a country by country basis:
      Section I - The Export Order
      Section II - Export Markets - regulations, documentation, business travel
      Section III - Export Know-How
      Section IV - Communications
      Section V - Information Sources/Services
      Section VI - Transportation Data/Services

Dun and Bradstreet International.

183 **Foreign Business Practices**. Information on foreign business practices such as patent and trademark protection, foreign licensing and joint ventures, the resolution of trade and investment disputes and tax benefits for U.S. exporters.

U.S. Department of Commerce, 1985. Su Doc #C61.2:

184 **Foreign Commerce Handbook.**   Information pertaining to all aspects of international business, including trade terms and organizations.

International Division, U.S. Chamber of Commerce, 1981.

185 **Guide to Documentary Credit Operations.**   Explains the role of documentary credits in international trade and shows how they work in practice.

ICC (International Chamber of Commerce) Publishing Corporation, Inc., 1985.

186 **Guide to Incoterms.**   Graphically explains the respective obligations of buyer and seller when using one of the Incoterms in a commercial transaction.   Diagrams and illustrations.

ICC (International Chamber of Commerce) Publishing Corporation, Inc., 1980.

187 **Incoterms.**   Defines universally used trade terms adopted in 1953, 1967, and 1968 and incorporates two new terms adopted in 1980.

ICC Publishing Corporation, Inc.

188 **International Countertrade: A Guide for Managers and Executives.**   Descriptions of countertrade practices, U.S. regulations relating to countertrade, and countertrade support services.   Also country-by-country applications of countertrade.

International Trade Administration, U.S. Department of Commerce, 1984.

189 **International Trade Reporter.**   Regularly updated. Country-by-country surveys of international trade situation, trade and exchange controls, and methods of handling export shipments.

Bureau of National Affairs, Inc.

190 **The Official Export Guide.**   Annual.   Provides information on all the world ports, trade regulations, export documentation, international financing, documentary requirements and other information needed to conduct export trade operations.

North American Publishing Company.

191 **Reference Book for World Traders**. Monthly. Information needed to execute export and import transactions with all foreign countries. Lists trade organizations, credit information agencies, banks, customs brokers, advertising agencies, and attorneys, as well as export documentation requirements.

Croner Publications.

192 **U.S. Export Weekly**. Weekly. Current developments affecting U.S. exports, including trade legislation, foreign exchanges, financing activities and arrangements, and economic conditions.

Bureau of National Affairs, Inc.

193 **United States International Trade Reports**. Continuously up-dated. Decisions of the U.S. Court of International Trade and the Court of Customs and Patent Appeals.

Oceana Publications, Inc.

194 **What Do I Do Now?: An Export Primer**. A basic guide for the beginner in exporting.

Global Risk Assessment, Inc., 2nd Edition, 1984.

VII
Promotional
and Financing Facilities

195 **American Export Marketer**. Monthly. Current information on export support services, taxes and export controls, exchange rates, product marketing opportunities, and economic and political developments affecting exporting.

The American Export Marketer.

196 **American Overseas Business and Travel Guide**. Annual. Hotels, restaurants, night clubs, shops, tourist information offices, consumer goods manufacturers, trade fairs and exhibitions of Eastern and Western Europe.

American Overseas Tourist Service of New York, Inc.

197 **Business Asia**. Weekly. Newsletter which offers short articles on economy, banking, management, licensing, etc. for Asian regions.

Business International Corporation.

198 **Business Eastern Europe**. Weekly. Newsletter which offers short articles on economy, banking, management, licensing, etc. for Eastern European regions.

Business International Corporation.

199 **Business Europe**. Weekly. Newsletter which offers short articles on economy, interest rates, investment, marketing personnel, currency, management, etc. for European regions.

Business International Corporation.

200 **Business International**. Weekly. Newsletter which offers short articles on capital sources, codes of conduct, currency, economy, exporting, foreign trade, management, marketing.

Business International Corporation.

201 **Business International Money Report**. Weekly. Newsletter which offers short articles on accounting, capital sources, stock and bond financing, Eurobonds, currency, financial techniques, etc.

Business International Corporation.

202 **Business Latin America**. Weekly. Newsletter which offers short articles on commodities, economy, industry, personnel and labor, importing, investing, etc. for Latin American regions.

Business International Corporation.

203 **Chase Guide to Government Export Credit Agencies**. Describes and compares government export credit programs of various nations and explains how exporters can utilize those programs.

World Information Corporation (Chase Manhattan Bank), 1985.

204 **Dynamics of Trade Finance**. Overview of the workings of international trade and finance. Topics include: Mechanics of trade financing, documentary collections, commercial letter of credit, bank undertakings, export factoring, foreign exchange, etc.

The Chase Manhattan Bank, 1984.

205 **Export Advisory Reference Manual**. Annual. A handbook containing information on export credit and collections, documentation, import/export regulations, government financing and insurance programs.

Chemical Bank - Export Advisory Service.

206 **Export Credit Financing Systems in OECD Member Countries**. A comparative summary of export credit financing systems in member countries of the

Organization for Economic Cooperation and Development.

Organization for Economic Cooperation and Development, 1982.

207 **Export Financing: A Handbook of Sources and Techniques.**
A handbook detailing new ways of financing exports using less traditional sources and techniques and revealing the less obvious risks and benefits.

Financial Executives Research Foundation (FERF), 1985.

208 **Export Promotion Calendar.** Quarterly. Lists U.S. trade promotion events held abroad. Indexed by product, giving data and location of each event.

U.S. Department of Commerce, International Trade Administration.

209 **Financing and Insuring Exports: A User's Guide to Eximbank and FCIA Programs.** A basic guide to the export financing and export credit insurance programs of the U.S. Export-Import Bank and the Foreign Credit Insurance Association.

Export-Import Bank of the U.S., 1985.

210 **Financing Foreign Operations.** Monthly. Detailed data on sources and methods of financing business operations in foreign areas. Organized into the following sections:
     I - Techniques for Financing
    II - Cross-Border Financing
   III - Domestic Financing
           Africa, Middle East
           Asia
           Europe
           Latin America
           North America

Business International Corporation.

211 **Foreign Exchange Yearbook.** Annual. A listing of daily foreign exchange and Eurocurrency deposit rates for leading world currencies with a commentary on international developments.

Woodhead-Faulkner, Limited.

212 **GreenBook - International Directory of Marketing Research Houses and Services**. Annual. Listing of market research firms - includes name, address, phone number, principal executives, type of services offered. Alphabetical listing, then late listings and geographic/telephone listings; personnel index and computer programs listing.

New York Chapter of the American Marketing Association.

213 **Guide to Financing Exports**. Basics on credit, payment terms, organizations offering financing and risk protection.

U.S. Department of Commerce, 1985.   Su Doc #C61.8:

214 **Insurance in International Finance**. Reports on sources of export credit insurance, foreign investment guarantees, and export financing.

International Reports, Inc., 1980.

215 **International Commercial Financing Intelligence**. Bi-weekly. Covers key developments in trade and international trade financing.

International Reports, Inc.

216 **International Finance Handbook**. 2 Volumes. Comprehensive handbook on international finance. Gives practical guidance on foreign exchange management, international money and capital markets, international financing techniques and sources.

John Wiley and Sons, Inc., 1983.

217 **Investing, Licensing and Trading Conditions Abroad**. Regularly updated. Detailed information on state role in industry; rules of competition; price controls; licensing; remittability of funds; corporate taxes; personal taxes; incentives; capital sources; labor; foreign trade. Covers all countries and regions of the world.

Business International Corporation.

218 **1985 Chase Guide to Government Export Credit Agencies**. Information on export credit programs throughout the world.

The World Information Corporation (Chase Manhattan Bank), 1985.

219 **Pick's Currency Yearbook**. Annual. Offers a complete review of exchange rate and currency developments throughout the world, including restrictions, black market position, etc. Also a description of prices and movements of gold in international trading centers.

Pick Publishing Corporation.

220 **Polk's World Bank Directory: International Section**. Alphabetical index to banks - indexed according to continent, then country. Lists address, officers, current statement, correspondents.

R.L. Polk and Company, 1982.

221 **Rand McNally International Bankers Directory**. Updated six times a year. U.S. and International Bank Listings - address, statement of condition, correspondents, cable number, chair; manager, etc.

Rand McNally and Company.

222 **Reference Book for World Traders**. Monthly. Information needed to execute export and import transactions with all foreign countries. Lists trade organizations, credit information agencies, banks, customs brokers, advertising agencies, and attorneys, as well as export documentation requirements.

Croner Publications.

223 **Tax Free Trade Zones of the World**. 3 Volumes. Updated periodically. Free trade zones, free ports, transit zones, free perimeters, and other special facilities in nearly 400 areas throughout the world that offer the most favorable tax treatments.

Matthew Bender and Co., Inc.

VIII
Political Data
and Political Risk Assessments

224 **Army Area Handbooks**. Irregular. Each handbook in this
series discusses a particular foreign country's social
institutions, political system, and economic structure.
All handbooks include bibliographies providing
references to additional sources of information on the
country.

United States Army.

225 **Business Asia**. Weekly. Newsletter which offers short
articles on economy, banking, management, licensing,
etc. for Asian regions.

Business International Corporation.

226 **Business Eastern Europe**. Weekly. Newsletter which
offers short articles on economy, banking, management,
licensing, etc. for Eastern European regions.

Business International Corporation.

227 **Business Environment Risk Information**. Tri-annual.
Assessments of political risks, economic trends,
currency convertibility, business operating conditions,
and profit opportunities for each of 48 countries.

IRM (International Research and Marketing), Inc.

228 **Business Europe**. Weekly. Newsletter which offers short
articles on economy, interest rates, investment,
marketing, personnel, currency, management, etc. for

European regions.

Business International Corporation.

229 **Business   International**.   Weekly.   Newsletter   which
offers   short   articles   on   capital   sources,   codes   of
conduct, currency, economy, exporting, foreign trade,
management, marketing.

Business International Corporation.

230 **Business   Latin   America**.   Weekly.   Newsletter   which
offers short articles on commodities, economy, industry,
personnel and labor, importing, investment, etc. for
Latin American regions.

Business International Corporation.

231 **The   Encyclopedia   of   the   Third   World**.   3   Volumes.
Provides a compact, balanced and objective description
of the dominant political, economic and social systems
of 122 countries of the world.

Facts on File, Inc., 1982.

232 **Europa Yearbook - A World Survey**. Annual. 2 Volumes.
    Volume I
Part   I - International Organizations - activities, address,
etc.
Part   II - Europe
Part III - Afghanistan - Burundi
    Volume II
Cameroon - Zimbabwe
Includes history, government, economic affairs, etc. of
individual countries.

Europa Publications, Limited.

233 **International Country Risk Guide**. Monthly. Country-by-
country analyses of political, commercial, and financial
risks.

International Reports, Inc.

234 **Managing and Evaluating Country Risk**. Covers the nature
of country risk and types of business decisions affected
by such risk.   Indicates how corporations use country-
risk ratings in decision-making and provides ratings for
57 major countries.

Business International Corporation, 1981.

235 **OECD Economic Surveys**. Annual. Economic surveys of
each of the 24 OECD member countries, containing
information on current trends in demand and output,
prices and wages, foreign trade and payments, economic
policies, and future economic prospects.

Organization for Economic Cooperation and Development.

236 **Political Climate for International Business**. Annual.
Ranks some 80 countries of the world by risk criteria,
including government stability and social unrest.

Frost and Sullivan, Inc.

237 **Political Handbook of the World**. Alphabetical by
country: political states, area, population, major
urban centers, official language, monetary unit, ruling
party; government and politics, political parties;
legislature; cabinet, etc.

Published for the Center for Social Analysis of the
State University of New York at Binghamton and for the
Council on Foreign Relations by
McGraw Hill Book Company, 1981.

238 **U.S.S.R. Facts and Figures Annual**. Annual. Includes
government, communist party, demography, armed forces,
economy, energy, industrial production, industries,
agriculture, foreign trade and aid, health, education,
welfare, culture and communications, transportation,
institutions.

Academic International Press.

239 **World Political Risk Forecasts**. Monthly. Economic data
and assessments of political risk for 70 countries.

Frost and Sullivan, Inc., 1984.

IX
Bibliographies, Directories, and Indexes

240 **American Statistics Index (ASI).** Monthly. Identifies, indexes and provides abstract information for the publications of more than 400 U.S. government organizations and agencies.

Congressional Information Service, Inc.

241 **Business International Index.** Quarterly and cumulative. Index to **Business International's** complete publishing system of international business information.

Business International Corporation.

242 **Business Periodicals Index.** Quarterly. Indexes all major business and economic journals and periodicals.

The H.W. Wilson Company.

243 **Business Publications Index and Abstracts.** Monthly with annual accumulations. Subject and author index with abstracts of periodical articles, selected books, and conference proceedings.

Gale Research Company.

244 **CIS Index.** Monthly. Indexes and abstracts all publications of the Congress of the United States, including hearings, committee prints, congressional reports and documents.

Congressional Information Service, Inc.

245 **The Conference Board - Cumulative Index.** Annual. Guide
to current Conference Board research. Indexed by
subject. Major areas of research include: business
economics, public affairs, international operations,
personnel, marketing, finance, administration.

The Conference Board, Inc.

246 **Current African Directories.** Irregular. Guide to
directories and other sources of business information
covering all countries of Africa.

CBD Research, Ltd.

247 **Current European Directories.** Irregular. Guide to
international, national and specialized directories
covering all countries of Europe.

CBD Research, Ltd.

248 **The Dow Jones - Irwin Business and Investment Almanac.**
Annual. Includes business in review (daily basis);
breakdown of industries - textiles, metals, energy;
financial statements by industry; stock market,
commodities markets. Includes some international.

Dow Jones - Irwin.

249 **Europa Yearbook - A World Survey.** Annual. 2 Volumes.
      Volume I
Part   I - International organizations - activities,
      address, etc.
Part   II - Europe
Part III - Afghanistan - Burundi
      Volume II
Cameroon - Zimbabwe
Includes history, government, economic affairs, etc. of
individual countries.

Europa Publications, Limited.

250 **Exporter's Encyclopedia.** Annual. Provides the
following data on a country-by-country basis:
      Section I - The Export Order
      Section   II - Export Markets - regulations,
         documentation, business travel
      Section III - Export Know-How
      Section IV - Communications
      Section V - Information Sources/Services

Section VI - Transportation Data/Services

Dun and Bradstreet International.

251 **F & S International**. Annual. Indexes current articles
on foreign companies and industries. Arranged in three
sections:
Section 1 - industries and products
Section 2 - countries
Section 3 - companies

Predicasts, Inc.

252 **FINDEX: The Directory of Market Research Reports,
Studies, and Surveys**. Annual with supplements. Guide
to market and business research reports.   Describes
consumer and industry studies and surveys. Arranged by
industry with geographic index.

FIND/SVP.

253 **F & S Index Europe**. Annual. Indexes current articles
on European companies and industries. Arranged in 3
sections:
Section 1 - Industries and products - arranged by SIC
code
Section 2 - Entries arranged by region
Section 3 - Companies - alphabetical

Predicasts, Inc.

254 **GreenBook   -   International Directory of Marketing
Research Houses and Services**. Annual. Listing of
market research firms - includes name, address, phone
number, principal executives, type of services offered.
Alphabetical   listing,   then   late   listings   and
geographic/telephone listings; personnel index and
computer programs listing.

New York Chapter of the American Marketing Association.

255 **International Bibliography, Information, Documentation**.
Quarterly.   Subject classifications: commerce and
business, culture, international economic relations,
international   law,   international   organization,
international relations, etc.

Unipub (A Xerox Publishing Co.).

256 **The International Executive**. Quarterly. Annotated
bibliography of current books and journal articles
relating to all aspects of international business as
well as economic and business conditions in various
regions of the world.

American Graduate School of International Management.

257 **International Marketing: An Annotated Bibliography**.
Identifies sources of information on the environment,
customers, competition, and channels in international
markets.

American Marketing Association, 1985.

258 **International Organizations**. (Volume 4 of **The
Encyclopedia of Associations**). Annual. A guide to
trade, professional and other non-profit organizations
that are international in scope. Describes each
organization's aims and activities and its information
resources.

Gale Research Company.

259 **International Yearbook and Statesmen's Who's Who**.
Annual.
Part I - International and National Organizations
    United Nations
    Specialized Agencies of the United Nations
    Affiliated Agencies of the United Nations
    Inter-Governmental Organizations
    Other International and National Organizations
Part II - Organization of foreign ministries of Great
Powers, Metric Conversions, etc.

Kelly's Directories.

260 **Monthly Catalog of U.S. Government Publications**.
Monthly. Indexes all publications of the U.S.
government.

Superintendent of Documents, U.S. Government Printing
Office.

261 **Public Affairs Information Service (PAIS) Index**.
Quarterly. Indexes all major business and social
science publications as well as many government
publications.

Public Affairs Information Service, Inc.

262 **Sources** **of** **European** **Economic** **Information**. Bibliography
    of European business publications, including a summary
    of the contents of each publication.

    Ballinger Publishing Company, 1983.

263 **Statistics**   **-**   **Africa**.   Irregular.   Describes
    organizations and publications providing statistical
    information for economic, social and market research for
    all countries of Africa.

    CBD Research, Ltd.

264 **Statistics**   **-**   **America**.   Irregular.   Describes
    organizations and publications providing statistical
    information for economic, social and market research in
    North, Central and South America.

    CBD Research, Ltd.

265 **Statistics** **-** **Asia** **and** **Australasia**. Irregular.
    Describes organizations and publications providing
    statistical information for economic, social and market
    research for all countries in Asia, Australasia and
    Oceania.

    CBD Research, Ltd.

266 **Statistics**   **-**   **Europe**.   Irregular.   Describes
    organizations and publications providing statistical
    information for economic, social and market research in
    Western and Eastern Europe.

    CBD Research, Ltd.

267 **Statistics** **Sources**. A subject guide to data on
    industrial, business, social, educational, financial;
    and other topics for the U.S. and internationally
    oriented individuals. Alphabetical - includes
    individual country sources.

    Gale Research Company, 1984.

268 **UNDOC:**   **Current**   **Index**.   Annual.   United Nations
    Documents Index
        Vol. 1 - checklist of documents

> official records
> sales publications
> Vol. 2 - subject index

United Nations.

269 **Wall Street Journal Index**. Monthly with annual accumulations. Indexes all topics appearing in the Wall Street Journal.

Dow Jones and Company, Inc.

270 **Washington's Best Kept Secrets: A U.S. Government Guide to International Business.** Updated with regular supplements. Identifies the U.S. government agencies which provide information and assistance to American businesses wishing to expand into foreign markets and tells how to secure such information and assistance.

John Wiley and Sons, 1983.

271 **World-Wide Chamber of Commerce Directory**. Annual. A complete list of Chambers of Commerce in the U.S. and abroad, foreign embassies and consulates in the U.S., United States embassies and consulates throughout the world, and foreign consular offices in the United States.

Johnson Publishing Company, Inc.

272 **Yearbook of International Organizations**. Irregular. 14,784 groups indexed. Contains organization names (in their working language); name keywords; initials or abbreviations; country and town of secretariat location. Contains brief history, aim, structure, activities, publications, etc.

Union of International Associations and International Chamber of Commerce.

X
Dictionaries

273 **Dictionary** **of** **Shipping/International** **Trade** **Terms** **and** **Abbreviations**.

Witherby and Company, Limited
1st Edition, 1976.
2nd Edition, 1982.

274 **Dictionnaire** **anglais-francais** **et** **lexique** **francais-anglais**. English-French dictionary of political, legal and economic terms.

Flammarion, 1978.

275 **Guide** **to** **Incoterms**. Graphically explains the respective obligations of buyer and seller when using one of the Incoterms in a commercial transaction. Diagrams and illustrations.

ICC (International Chamber of Commerce) Publishing Corporation, Inc.

276 **Incoterms**. Defines universally used trade terms adopted in 1953, 1967, 1968 and incorporates two new terms adopted in 1980.

ICC (International Chamber of Commerce) Publishing Corporation, Inc.

277 **Key** **Words** **in** **International** **Trade**. Translates nearly 1000 technical English words dealing with international trade into German, Spanish, French and Italian.

Complete with indexes.

ICC (International Chamber of Commerce) Publishing Corporation, Inc.

278 **The Multilingual Commercial Dictionary**. A collection of the most commonly used business terms in six languages: English, French, German, Spanish, Italian and Portuguese.

Facts on File, Inc., 1978.

279 **Reuters Glossary of International Economic and Financial Terms**. Brief description of important financial, marketing, accounting and economic terms.

Coward-McCann, Inc., 1982.

280 **Rosenberg Dictionary of Business and Management**. Contains brief definition of terms (letter of credit, bill of lading), table of equivalents; metric conversions; interest tables, foreign exchange. Includes accounting, advertising, export-import, etc.

John Wiley and Sons, Inc., 1978.

281 **The VNR Dictionary of Business and Finance**. Includes terms used in international business: letter of credit, eurodollars, European Monetary System, free trade zone.

Van Nostrand Reinhold Company, 1980.

XI
Databases for International Marketers

Many of the reference sources discussed in earlier sections are available through computerized databases. In addition, there is some pertinent marketing data available only online.

The advantage of a computerized search of data is speed, efficiency, and specificity. By entering key words or codes, you can retrieve data directly related to your area of interest.

Access to these databases can be made by an individual or corporation who contracts or subscribes to a database service. Unless you are planning to make extensive use of the service, it is very expensive. A more cost efficient method would be to inquire about database searching at a large public or academic library. Most of these institutions have established contracts with major database vendors and have experienced searchers who can conduct a search in a timely and cost efficient manner. Generally, the only charge to you is the actual cost of the search; some libraries do attach a small service fee.

Listed below are some of the major databases of interest to those in international marketing. For those with a print counterpart described earlier, the entry number is given. There are also many directories of databases available in bookstores and libraries describing these and other databases in greater detail.

282 Name of Database: **ABI/INFORM**

Coverage or Contents: Covers all areas of business management and administration. The primary emphasis is on general decision sciences information applicable to

many types of businesses and industries. Also contained
are specific product and industry information.

Producer: Data Courier, Inc.
           620 South Fifth Street
           Louisville, Kentucky 40202
           (502) 582-4111
           (800) 626-2823

283 Name of Database: **CANADIAN BUSINESS PERIODICALS INDEX**
    (CBPI)

Coverage or Contents: Maintains citations to 170
Canadian English-language business, industry, and trade
publications.   Coverage   includes   new   product
introductions, corporate activities, finance, computer
science, real estate, taxation, general management,
service industries and utilities.

Producer: Micromedia Limited
           144 Front Street, West
           Toronto, Ontario, Canada M5J 1G2
           (416) 593-5211

284 Name of Database: **CIS/INDEX**

Coverage or Contents: Provides citations and abstracts
of virtually every publication produced by approximately
300 House,   Senate,   and   Joint   Committees   and   sub-
committees of Congress since 1970.   Subject areas
include almost all business, economic, and technology
topics.

Producer: Congressional Information Service, Inc. (CIS)
           7101 Wisconsin Avenue, Suite 900
           Washington, D.C.   20014
           (301) 654-1550

285 Name of Database: **DISCLOSURE II**

Coverage or Contents: Provides extracts of reports
filed with the Securities and Exchange Commission by
publicly owned companies.

Producer: Disclosure, Inc.
           5161 River Road
           Bethesda, Maryland 20816
           (301) 951-1300
           (800) 638-8076

286 Name of Database: **DOW JONES NEWS/RETRIEVAL SERVICE AND STOCK QUOTE REPORTER**

Coverage or Contents: Full-text news and articles from major financial publications. The Stock Quote Reporter maintains price quotations for most stock exchange companies.

Producer: Dow Jones & Company, Inc.
            Post Office Box 300
            Princeton, New Jersey 08540
            (800) 257-5114
            (600) 452-2000

287 Name of Database: **DUN'S FINANCIAL PROFILES**

Coverage or Contents: Maintains annual financial data for public and private companies.

Producer: Dun & Bradstreet, Inc.
            99 Church Street
            New York, New York 10007
            (212) 285-7000

288 Name of Database: **ENCYCLOPEDIA OF ASSOCIATIONS (EA)**

Coverage or Contents: Provides detailed information on several thousand trade associations, professional societies, labor unions, fraternal and patriotic organizations and similar types of groups consisting of voluntary members.

Producer: Gale Research Company
            Book Tower
            Detroit, Michigan 48226
            (313) 961-2242

289 Name of Database: **FOREIGN TRADERS INDEX (FTI)**

Coverage or Contents: Directory of manufacturers, service organizations, agent representatives, retailers, wholesalers, distributors and cooperatives in 130 countries outside the United States.

Producer: U.S. Department of Commerce
            Bureau of Export Development
            Commerce ITA/1033/FTI
            Washington, D.C. 20230
            (202) 377-2988

290 Name of Database: CPO MONTHLY CATALOG DATA BASE

Coverage or Contents: Data base equivalent of the
printed Monthly Catalog of U.S. Government Publications.

Producer: U.S. Government Printing Office
            Library Division
            5236 Eisenhower Avenue
            Alexandria, Virginia 22304
            (703) 557-2135

Entry #:   260

291 Name of Database: HARFAX

Coverage or Contents: References to over 14,000
industry data sources.

Producer: Harfax Data Base Publishing
            Post Office Box 281
            54 Fall Street
            Cambridge, Massachusetts 02138
            (617) 492-0670

292 Name of Database: THE INFORMATION BANK

Coverage or Contents: A comprehensive current-affairs
data base consisting of informative abstracts from many
major English-language publications.

Producer: The New York Times Information Service, Inc.
            Mt. Pleasant Office Park
            1719A Route 10
            Parsippany, New Jersey 0705438
            (201) 539-5850

293 Name of Database: INTERNATIONAL BUSINESS INTELLIGENCE
PROGRAM (B-I-P) INDEX

Coverage or Contents: Provides abstracts from four B-I-
P publications. Research Reports analyzes key changes
which will affect business and industry during the next
ten years.

Producer: SRI International
            333 Ravenswood Avenue
            Menlo Park, California 94025
            (415) 859-6300

294 <u>Name</u> <u>of</u> <u>Database</u>:   **INTERNATIONAL FINANCIAL STATISTICS (IFS)**

<u>Coverage</u> <u>or</u> <u>Contents</u>:. Collection of economic and financial statistics for the 150 member nations of the International Monetary Fund.

<u>Producer</u>:   International Monetary Fund (IMF)
             19th and H Street, N.W.
             Washington, D.C.   20431
             (202) 477-7000

<u>Entry</u> **#**:   054

295 <u>Name</u> <u>of</u> <u>Database</u>:   **MANAGEMENT CONTENTS**

<u>Coverage</u> <u>or</u> <u>Contents</u>:   Maintains current information on a variety of business and management related topics.

<u>Producer</u>:   Management Contents, Inc.
             2265 Carlson Drive, Suite 5000
             Northbrook, Illinois 60062
             (312) 564-1006
             (800) 323-5354

296 <u>Name</u> <u>of</u> <u>Database</u>:   **NATIONAL NEWSPAPER INDEX (NNI)**

<u>Coverage</u> <u>or</u> <u>Contents</u>:   Provides front to back page indexing of the <u>Christian</u> <u>Science</u> <u>Monitor</u>, the <u>New</u> <u>York</u> <u>Times</u> and the <u>Wall</u> <u>Street</u> <u>Journal</u>.

<u>Producer</u>:   Information Access Corporation
             404 Sixth Avenue
             Menlo Park, California 94025
             (415) 367-7171
             (800) 227-8431

297 <u>Name</u> <u>of</u> <u>Database</u>:   **NEWSPAPER INDEX (NDEX)**

<u>Coverage</u> <u>or</u> <u>Contents</u>:   Maintains citations to local, state, national and international news on all business related topics.

<u>Producer</u>:   Bell & Howell
             Micro Photo Division
             Old Mansfield Road
             Wooster, Ohio 44691
             (216) 264-6666
             (800) 321-9881

298 Name of Database: **PTS INDEXES**

Coverage or Contents: Covers both domestic and international company, product and industry information.

Producer: Predicasts, Inc.
200 University Circle Research Center
11001 Cedar Avenue
Cleveland, Ohio 44106
(216) 795-3000
(800) 321-6388

Entry #: 046, 251

299 Name of Database: **PTS INTERNATIONAL FORECASTS ABSTRACTS**

Coverage or Contents: Abstracts of published forecasts with historical data for all counties of the United States.

Producer: Predicasts, Inc.
200 University Circle Research Center
11001 Cedar Avenue
Cleveland, Ohio 44106
(216) 795-3000
(800) 321-6388

300 Name of Database: **PTS INTERNATIONAL TIME SERIES**

Coverage or Contents: Approximately 2,500 forecast time series consisting of 50 key series for 50 major countries of the world. Time series include historical data and projected consensus of published forecasts through 1990.

Producer: Predicasts, Inc.
200 University Circle Research Center
11001 Cedar Avenue
Cleveland, Ohio 44106
(216) 795-3000
(800) 321-6388

301 Name of Database: **PTS PROMPT**

Coverage or Contents: Abstracts significant information appearing in thousands of newspapers, business magazines, government reports, trade journals, bank letters and international reports.

Producer: Predicasts, Inc.
200 University Circle Research Center

11001 Cedar Avenue
Cleveland, Ohio 44106
(216) 795-3000
(800) 321-6388

Entry #:   046, 251

302 Name of Database: **TRADE AND INDUSTRY INDEX**

Coverage or Contents: An index to business journals
relating to trade, industry and commerce.

Producer: Information Access Corporation
404 Sixth Avenue
Menlo Park, California 94025
(415) 367-7171
(800) 227-8431

303 Name of Database: **TRADE OPPORTUNITIES WEEKLY**

Coverage or Contents: Includes information, both
current and historical, on export opportunities
overseas.

Producer: U.S. Department of Commerce
Trade Facilitation Information & Services Division
ITA/1033/FTI
Washington, D.C.   20230
(202) 377-2988

Entry #:   105

304 Name of Database: **U.S. EXPORTS**

Coverage or Contents: Maintains export statistics for
all commodities in dollar value and shipping weight,
reflecting both government and non-government exports of
domestic and foreign merchandise from the U.S. and
territories to foreign countries.

Producer: U.S. Census Bureau
Foreign Trade Division
Washington, D.C.   20233
(301) 763-5140

Appendix A
Directory of Publishers

Academic International Press
Box 1111
Gulf Breeze, FL   32561

Adweek
820 Second Avenue
New York, NY   10017
(212) 661-8080

The American Export Marketer
10076 Boca Entrada Blvd.
Boca Raton, FL   33433

American Graduate School of International Management
Campus Box 1700
Glendale, AZ   85306
(602) 978-7249

American Management Associations
135 West 50th Street
New York, NY   10020

American Marketing Association
250 South Wacker Drive
Chicago, IL   60606
(312) 648-0536

American Overseas Tourist
Service of New York, Inc.
663 Fifth Avenue
New York, NY   10022

Asia Cable
P.O. Box 3456
Portland, OR   97208

Ballinger Publishing Company
54 Church Street
Cambridge, MA   02138
(617) 492-0670

Matthew Bender and Co., Inc.
P.O. Box 989
Dept D.M.
Albany, NY   12201

Bureau of National Affairs, Inc.
1231 25th Street, N.W.
Washington, D.C.   20037
(202) 452-4379

Business International Corporation
One Dag Hammarskjold Plaza
New York, NY   10017

Capital Publications, Inc.
1300 N. 17th St.
Arlington, VA   22209

CBD Research, Ltd.
154 High Street
Beckenham
Kent BR3 1EA
United Kingdom
(01) 650-7745

The Chase Manhattan Bank
One World Trade Center, 78th Floor
New York, NY   10048

Chemical Bank - Export Advisory Service
52 Broadway
New York, NY   10004

Commerce Clearing House, Inc.
4025 W. Peterson Avenue
Chicago, IL   60646
(312) 583-8500

Commodity Research Bureau, Inc.
One Liberty Plaza
New York, NY   10006

The Conference Board, Inc.
845 Third Avenue
New York, NY   10022
(212) 759-0900

Congressional Information Service, Inc.
4520 East - West Highway

Bethesda, MD 20814
(301) 654-1550

Coward-McCann Inc.
200 Madison Avenue
New York, NY 10016
(212) 576-8900

Croner Publications
211 Jamaica Avenue
Queens Village, NY 11428
(212) 464-0866

Croom Helm Ltd.
51 Washington Street
Dover, NH 03820
(603) 749-5038

Dow Jones and Company, Inc.
P.O. Box 300
Princeton, NJ 08540
(609) 452-1511

Dow Jones-Irwin
1818 Ridge Road
Homewood, IL 60430
(312) 798-6000

Dun and Bradstreet International
99 Church Street
New York, NY 10007

Elsevier Science Pubishers
Journal Information Center
52 Vanderbilt Avenue
New York, NY 10017
(212) 370-5520

Euromonitor Publications, Ltd.
87-88 Turnmill Street
London EC1M 5QW
England

Europa Publications, Limited
c/o Unipub
Customer Services Department
P.O. Box 1222
Ann Arbor, MI 48106
(800) 521-8110

Export-Import Bank of the U.S.
811 Vermont Avenue, N.W.
Washington, D.C. 20571

Facts on File, Inc.
Order Department
460 Park Avenue South
New York, NY 10016
(212) 683-2244

Far Eastern Economic Review, Ltd.
CPO Box 160
Hong Kong

Financial Executives Research Foundation (FERF)
10 Madison Avenue
P.O. Box 1938
Morristown, NJ 07906
(201) 898-4600

Flammarion
26 Rue Racine
F-75278
Paris Cedex 06
France

Food and Agriculture Organization of the United Nations
c/o Unipub
A Xerox Publishing Company
205 E. 42nd Street
New York, NY 10017
(212) 916-1659

Frost and Sullivan, Inc.
106 Fulton Street
New York, NY 10038
(212) 233-1080

Gale Research Company
Book Tower
Detroit, MI 48226
(313) 961-2242

General Agreement on Tariffs and Trade (GATT)
c/o Unipub
A Xerox Publishing Company
205 E. 42nd Street
New York, NY 10017
(212) 916-1659

Global Risk Assessment, Inc.
Publications Division
3638 University Avenue, Suite 215
Riverside, CA 92501
(714) 788-0672

Graham and Trotman, Limited
Sterling House

66 Wilton Road
London SW1V 1DE
England

International Chamber of Commerce
ICC Publishing Corporation
156 5th Avenue
New York, NY   10010

International Monetary Fund
700 19th Street, N.W.
Washington, D.C.   20431
(202) 477-3086

International Reports, Inc.
200 Park Avenue South
New York, NY   10003
(212) 477-0003

IRM (International Research and Marketing), Inc.
BERI Marketing Representatives
The Plaza, 2 West 59th Street
New York, NY   10019

The Johns Hopkins University Press
Baltimore, MD   21218
(301) 338-7864

Johnson International Publishing Company, Inc.
386 Park Avenue South
New York, NY   10016

Johnson Publishing Company, Inc.
P.O. Box 990
1880 S. 57 Ct.
Boulder, CO   80306
(303) 443-1576

Kelly's Directories, Ltd.
Windsor Court
East Grinstead House
East Grinstead
West Sussex RH19 1XB

Kogan Page, Limited
120 Pentonville Road
London N1 9JN
United Kingdom
(01) 837-7851

McGraw Hill Book Company
1221 Avenue of the Americas
New York, NY   10020
(212) 512-2000

Moody's Investors Service, Inc.
99 Church Street
New York, NY 10007
(212) 553-0300

New York Chapter, Inc.
American Marketing Association
420 Lexington Avenue
New York, NY 10017

Newspaper Enterprise Association, Inc.
200 Park Avenue
New York, NY 10166
(212) 557-9651

North American Publishing Company
401 North Broad Street
Philadelphia, PA 19108
(215) 238-5300

Oceana Publications, Inc.
Dobbs Ferry, NY 10522
(914) 693-1733

Organization for Economic Cooperation and Development (OECD)
1750 Pennsylvania Avenue, N.W.
Suite 1207
Washington, D.C. 20006
(202) 724-1857

Pick Publishing Corporation
21 West Street
New York, NY 10006
(212) 425-0591

R.L. Polk and Company
6065 Atlantic Blvd., Suite E
Norcross, GA 30071
(404) 447-1280

Predicasts, Inc.
200 University Circle Center
11001 Cedar Avenue
Cleveland, OH 44106
(216) 795-3000

Price Waterhouse and Company
1251 Avenue of the Americas
New York, NY 10020

Public Affairs Information Service, Inc.
New York Public Library
Economic and Public Affairs Division

10 W. 40 Street
New York, NY   10008
(212) 736-6629

Rand McNally and Company
P.O. Box 7600
Chicago, IL   60680
(312) 673-9100

S.J. Rundt Associates
130 E. 63rd Street
New York, NY   10021

Societe Didot-Bottin (Paris)
28 Rue du Docteur Finlay
Paris, France

Superintendent of Documents
U.S. Government Printing Office
Washington, D.C.   20402

Taylor and Francis, Inc.
242 Cherry Street
Philadelphia, PA   19106
(215) 238-0939

Thomas International Publishing
P.O. Box 6376
Washington, D.C.   20015
(301) 657-2910

Twin Coast Newspapers, Inc.
110 Wall Street
New York, NY   10005

**Union of International Associations and International
Chamber of Commerce**
ICC Publishing Corporation, Inc.
125 E. 23rd Street, Suite 300
New York, NY   10010

Unipub
A Xerox Publishing Company
205 E. 42nd Street
New York, NY   10017
(212) 916-1659

United Nations
Sales Section, Publishing Division
New York, NY   10017
(212) 754-2940

United States Army
c/o Superintendent of Documents

U.S. Government Printing Office
Washington, D.C.   20402

U.S. Central Intelligence Agency
c/o Superintendent of Documents
U.S. Government Printing Office
Washington, D.C.   20402

U.S. Chamber of Commerce
International Division
1615 H Street, N.W.
Washington, D.C.   20062
(2102) 659-6000

U.S. Department of Agriculture
Foreign Agricultural Service
Room 4945 South Building
Washington, D.C.   20250

U.S. Department of Commerce
Superintendent of Documents
U.S. Government Printing Office
Washington, D.C.   20402
or
Local District Office of the Department of Commerce

Van Nostrand Reinhold Company
Division of Litton Educational Publishing, Inc.
135 W. 50th Street
New York, NY   10020
(212) 265-8700

John Wiley and Sons, Inc.
605 Third Avenue
New York, NY   10158
(212) 850-6418

The H.W. Wilson Company
950 University Avenue
Bronx, NY   10452
(212) 588-8400

Witherby and Company, Limited
5 Plantain Place
Crosby Row
London SE1 1YN
United Kingdom

Woodhead-Faulkner, Limited
51 Washington Street
Dover, NH   08320

The World Bank
Publications Unit

1818 H Street, N.W.
Washington, D.C.   20433
(202) 477-1234

The World Information Corporation
One World Trade Center, 78th Floor
New York, NY   10048

World Trade Academy Press, Inc.
50 East 42nd Street
New York, NY   10017
(212) 697-4999

World Trade Education Center
Cleveland State University
1983 East 24th Street
Cleveland, OH   44115

Appendix B
State Trade Contacts

Alabama

Ala. Devel. Office
State Capitol
Montgomery, AL   36130
(205) 263-0048

Ala. State Docks
P.O. Box 1588
Mobile, AL   36633
(205) 690-6113

Ala. World Trade Assn.
P.O. Box 1508
Mobile, AL   36633
(205) 431-9271

Center for Intl. Trade and
Commerce
Suite 131, 250 N. Water St.
Mobile, AL   36633
(205) 433-1151

Governor's Office of Intl.
Trade
P.O. Box 2939
Montgomery, AL   36105-0930
(205) 284-8722

Intrl. Trade Center, Univ.

of Alabama
P.O. Box 6186
University, AL   35486
(205) 348-7621

North Ala. Intl. Trade Assn.
P.O. Box 927
Huntsville, AL   35804
(205) 532-3570

U.S. Dept. of Commerce
2015 2nd Ave. N.
Birmingham, AL   35203
(205) 254-1331

Alaska

Alaska Dept. of Commerce &
Econ. Devel.
Pouch D
Juneau, AK   99811
(907) 465-2500

Alaska State Chamber of
Commerce
310 Second St.
Juneau, AK   99801
(907) 586-2323

Anchorage Chamber of Commerce
415 F St.
Anchorage, AK   99501
(907) 272-2401

Consular Corps of Ariz.
8331 E. Rose Lane
Scottsdale, AZ   85253
(602) 947-6011

Fairbanks Chamber of Commerce
First National Center
100 Cushman St.
Fairbanks, AK   99707
(907) 452-1105

Sunbelt World Trade Assn.
7119 Sabino Vista Circle
Tucson, AZ   85715
(602) 866-0364

U.S. Dept. of Commerce (ITA)
701 C St., Box 32
Anchorage, AK   99513
(907) 271-5041

U.S. Dept. of Commerce (ITA)
2750 Valley Bank Center
Phoenix, AZ   85073
(602) 261-3285

Arizona

Arkansas

Amer. Graduate School of Intl.
Management
Thunderbird Campus
Glendale, AZ   85306
(602) 978-7115

Ark. Assn. of Planning and
Devel.
Fed. Bldg.
Little Rock, AR   72201
(501) 378-5637

Ariz. District Export Council
Box 26685
Tucson, AZ   85726
(602) 748-7555

Ark. Exporters Round Table
1660 Union National Plaza
Little Rock, AR   72201
(501) 375-5377

Ariz.-Mex. Commission
P.O. Box 13564
Phoenix, AZ   85002
(602) 255-1345

Ark. Industrial Devel. Com.
One State Capital Mall
Little Rock, AR   72201
(501) 371-7678

Ariz. Office of Econ. Planning
and Devel.
1700 W. Washington, 4th Floor
Phoenix, AZ   85007
(602) 255-5371

District Export Council
Savers Bldg., Suite 635
Capital at Spring St.
Little Rock, AR   72201
(501) 378-5794

Ariz. World Trade Assn.
c/o Phoenix Chamber of
Commerce
34 W. Monroe, Suite 900
Phoenix, AZ   85003
(602) 254-5521

Intl. Trade Center
Univ. of Ark. at Little Rock
33rd and University
Little Rock, AR   72204
(501) 371-2992

U.S. Dept. of Commerce (ITA)
Savers Bldg., Suite 635
Capital at Spring St.
Little Rock, AR   72201
(501) 378-5794

World Trade Club of NE Ark.
P.O. Box 2566
Jonesboro, AR   72401
(501) 932-7550

California

Calif. Assn. of Port
Authorities
1510 14th St.
Sacramento, CA   95816
(916) 446-6339

Calif. Chamber of Commerce
Trade Dept.
1027 10th St.
P.O. Box 1736
Sacramento, CA   95808
(916) 444-6670

Calif. Council for Intl.
Trade
77 Jack London Sq., Suite L
Oakland, CA   94607
(415) 452-0770

Calif. Dept. of Commerce
Office of Business Devel.
1121 L St., Suite 600
Sacramento, CA   95814

Calif. State World Trade Com.
1121 L St., Suite 310
Sacramento, CA   95814
(916) 324-5511

Custom Brokers & Freight
Forwarders Assn.
303 World Trade Center
San Francisco, CA   94111
(415) 982-7788

Econ. Devel. Corp. of LA County
1052 W. 6th St., Suite 510
Los Angeles, CA   90017
(213) 482-5222

Export Managers Assn. of Calif.
10919 Vanowen St.
North Hollywood, CA   91605
(818) 985-1158

Foreign Trade Assn. of S. Cal.
350 S. Figueroa St., Rm. 226
Los Angeles, CA   90071
(213) 627-0634

Inland Intl. Trade Assn.
World Trade Center
W. Sacramento, CA   95691
(916) 371-8000

Intl. Bus. Assn., Long Beach
Area
Chamber of Commerce
100 Oceangate Plaza, Suite 50
Long Beach, CA   90802

Intl. Business Council
Century City Chamber of
Commerce
2020 Ave. of the Stars,
Plaza Level
Century City, CA   90067
(213) 553-4062

Intl. Managers' Assn. of
San Francisco
Custom House, P.O. Box 2425
San Francisco, CA   94126
(415) 981-6690

Intl. Marketing Assn. of
Orange County
Cal. State Fullerton,
Mktg. Dept.
Fullerton, CA   92634
(714) 773-2223

San Jose, CA   95150
(408) 998-7000

LA Area Chamber of Commerce
Intl. Commerce
404 S. Bixel St.
Los Angeles, CA   90017
(213) 629-0722

S. Calif. District Export
Council
11777 San Vicente Blvd.
Los Angeles, CA   90049
(213) 209-6707

N. Cal. District Export Council
450 Golden Gate Ave.
Box 36013
San Francisco, CA   94102
(415) 556-5868

U.S. Dept. of Commerce (ITA)
11777 San Vicente Blvd.
Los Angeles, CA   90047
(213) 209-6707

Oakland World Trade Assn.
1939 Harrison St.
Oakland, CA   94612
(415) 388-8829

U.S. Dept. of Commerce (ITA)
450 Golden Gate Ave.
San Francisco, CA   94102
(415) 556-5860

San Diego Chamber of Commerce
110 West "C" St., Suite 1600
San Diego, CA   92101
(619) 232-0124

U.S. Dept. of Commerce (ITA)
P.O. Box 81404
San Diego, CA   92138
(619) 293-5395

San Diego District Export
Council
P.O. Box 81404
San Diego, CA   92138
(619) 293-5395

U.S. Dept. of Commerce (ITA)
116 W. 4th St.
Santa Ana, CA   92701
(714) 836-2461

San Francisco Intl. Trade
Council
P.O. Box 6052
San Francisco, CA   94101
(415) 332-9100

U.S. Small Business Admin.
450 Golden Gate Ave.
San Francisco, CA   94102
(415) 556-9902

Valley Intl. Trade Assn.
c/o QUEP Secretarial Ser.
21133 Victory Blvd., Suite 221
Canoga Park, CA   91303
(818) 704-8626

San Francisco World Trade
Assn.
San Francisco Chamber of
Commerce
465 California St., 9th Floor
San Francisco, CA   94104
(415) 392-4511

World Trade Assn. of
Orange County
200 E. Sandpointe Ave.,
Suite 480
Santa Ana, CA   92707
(714) 549-4160

Santa Clara Valley World
Trade Assn.
P.O. Box 6178

World Trade Center Assn.
of San Diego
P.O. Box 81404
San Diego, CA   92138
(619) 298-6581

World Trade Council of San
Mateo County
4 West 4th Ave., Suite 501
San Mateo, CA   94402
(415) 342-7278

Colorado

Colo. Assn. of Commerce and
Industry
1390 Logan St.
Denver, CO   80202
(303) 831-7411

Colo. Div. of Commerce and
Devel.
1313 Sherman St., Rm. 523
Denver, CO   80203
(303) 866-2205

Denver Chamber of Commerce
1301 Welton St.
Denver, CO   80204
(303) 535-3211

Intl. Trade Assn. of Colo.
c/o U.S. Dept. of Commerce
721 19th St., Rm. 113
Denver, CO   80202
(303) 844-2900

U.S. Dept. of Commerce (ITA)
721 19th St., Rm. 113
Denver, CO   80202
(303) 844-2900

U.S. Small Business Admin.
1405 Curtis St.
Exec. Tower, 22nd Floor

Denver, CO   80202
(303) 844-5441

Connecticut

Bridgeport Foreign Trade Zone
45 Lyon Terrace, Rm. 212
Bridgeport, CT   06604
(203) 576-7221

Conn. Dept. of Econ. Devel.
210 Washington St.
Hartford, CT   06106
(203) 566-3842

Conn. District Export Council
450 Main St., Rm. 610B
Hartford, CT   06103
(203) 722-3530

Conn. Foreign Trade Assn.
c/o Manu. Assn. of S. Conn.
608 Ferry Blvd.
Stratford, CT   06497
(203) 762-1000

Conn. Intl. Trade Assn.
c/o Suisman & Blumenthal
P.O. Box 119
Hartford, CT   06141

(Greater) Hartford Foreign
Trade Zone
c/o Schuyler Corp.
999 Asylum Ave.
Hartford, CT   06105
(203) 728-0237

(Greater) Hartford Chamber of
Commerce
250 Constitution Plaza
Hartford, CT   06103
(203) 525-4451

Legal Assistance, Coordinator
111 Pearl St.

Hartford, CT   06103
(203) 547-1330

(Greater) New Haven Chamber
of Commerce
195 Church St.
New Haven, CT   06506
(203) 787-6735

Quinnipiac College
Mt. Carmel Ave.
Hamden, CT   06518
(203) 288-5251

Service Corps of Retired
Executives (SCORE)
1 Hartford Sq. W.
Hartford, CT   06103
(203) 722-3293

SW Area Commerce and Industry
Assn.
1 Landmark Sq., 2nd Floor
Stamford, CT   06901
(203) 359-3220

U.S. Dept. of Commerce (ITA)
450 Main St., Rm. 610B
Hartford, CT   06103
(203) 722-3530

U.S. Small Business Admin.
1 Hartford Sq. W.
Hartford, CT   06103
(203) 722-2544

West Conn. Intl. Trade Assn.
P.O. Box 787
Green Farms, CT   06436
(914) 478-3131

World Affairs Council
Hartford, CT   06105
(203) 236-5277

Delaware

Del. Devel. Office
P.O. Box 1401
Dover, DE   19903
(302) 736-4271

Del.-E. Pa. Export Council
9448 Fed. Bldg.
600 Arch St.
Philadelphia, PA   19106
(215) 597-2850

Del. State Chamber of Commerce
One Commerce Center, Suite 200
Wilmington, DE   19801
(302) 655-7221

Governor's Intl. Trade Council
State of Delaware
Legislative Hall
Dover, DE   19901
(302) 736-4136

Port of Wilmington
P.O. Box 1191
Wilmington, DE   19899
(302) 571-4600

U.S. Dept. of Commerce
9448 Fed. Bldg.
600 Arch St.
Philadelphia, PA   19106
(215) 597-2866

District of Columbia

Greater Washington Board of
Trade
1129 20th St. NW
Washington, D.C.   20036
(202) 857-5900

Montgomery County Ofc. of
Econ. Devel.
101 Monroe St., 15th Floor
Rockville, MD   20580
(301) 251-2345

U.S. Dept. of Commerce (ITA)
101 Monroe St., 15th Floor
Rockville, MD   20580
(301) 251-2345

Florida

Fla. Council of Intl. Devel.
2701 Le Jeune Rd., Suite 330
Coral Gables, FL   33134
(305) 448-4035

Fla. Customs Brokers &
Forwarders Assn. Inc.
P.O. Box 522022
Miami Springs, FL   33166
(305) 871-7177

Fla. Dept. of Commerce
Bureau of Intl. Trade
Collins Bldg.
107 W. Gaines St.
Tallahassee, FL   32304
(904) 488-6124

Fla. Dept. of Commerce
Caribbean Basin Devel. Center
2701 Le Jeune Rd., Suite 330
Coral Gables, FL   33134
(305) 446-8106

Fla. Dept. of Commerce
Latin American Trade
2701 Le Jeune Rd., Suite 330
Coral Gables, FL   33134
(305) 446-8106

Fla. District Export Council
c/o Miami Commerce District
Office
Fed. Bldg., Suite 224
51 SW. 1st Ave.
Miami, FL   33140
(305) 350-5267

Fla. Exporters & Importers
Assn. Inc.
P.O. Box 450648
Miami, FL   33145
(305) 446-6646

Fla. Intl. Bankers Assn.
800 Douglas Entrance, Suite 21
Coral Gables, FL   33134
(305) 446-6646

Fla. Small Business Devel.
Center
University of Florida
P.O. Box 32026
Pensacola, FL   32514

Ft. Lauderdale Area World
Trade Council
208 SE. 3rd Ave.
Ft. Lauderdale, FL   33302

Intl. Center of Fla.
800 Douglas Entrance
Suite 211
Coral Gables, FL   33134
(305) 446-6646

Jacksonville Intl. Trade Assn.
P.O. Box 329
Jacksonville, FL   32201
(904) 353-0300

(City of) Miami
Bureau of Intl. Trade
174 E. Flagler St., 7th Floor
Miami, FL   33133
(305) 579-3324

Okaloosa/Walton County Area
World Trade Council
P.O. Drawer 640
Fort Walton Beach, FL   32548
(904) 224-5151

Orlando World Trade Assn.
75 E. Ivanhoe Blvd.
Orlando, FL   32804
(305) 425-1234

Pensacola World Trade Council
40 N. Palasox St., Suite 400
Pensacola, FL   32501
(904) 438-4081

Space Coast World Trade Council
1005 E. Stawbridge Lane
Melbourne, FL   32901
(305) 724-5400

Sun Coast Export Council
St. Petersburg Area Chamber
of Commerce
P.O. Box 1371
St. Petersburg, FL   33731
(813) 821-4069

Tampa Bay Intl. Trade Council
P.O. Box 420
Tampa, FL   33601
(813) 228-7777

U.S. Dept. of Commerce (ITA)
Fed. Bldg., Suite 224
51 SW. 1st Ave.
Miami, FL   33140
(305) 350-5267

World Trade Council, Palm
Beach County
1983 PGA Blvd.
N. Palm Beach, FL   33408
(305) 832-5955

World Trade Council, Volusia
County
P.O. Box 5702
Daytona Beach, FL   32018
(904) 255-8131

Georgia

Ga. Dept. of Agriculture
328 Agriculture Bldg.
Atlanta, GA   30334
(404) 656-3740

Ga. Ports Authority
P.O. Box 2406
Savannah, GA   31412
(912) 964-1721

Ga. Dept. of Industry & Trade
1400 N. Omni Intl.
P.O. Box 1776
Atlanta, GA   30301
(404) 656-3571

Business Council of Ga.
575 N. Omni Intl.
Atlanta, GA   30335
(404) 223-2263

U.S. Dept. of Commerce (ITA)
Suite 600, 1365 Peachtree St.,
N.E.
Atlanta, GA   30309
(404) 881-7000

U.S. Dept. of Commerce (ITA)
27 E. Bay St.
P.O. Box 9746
Savannah, GA   31401
(912) 944-4204

Hawaii

Chamber of Commerce of Hawaii/
World Trade Assn.
735 Bishop St.
Honolulu, HI   96813
(808) 531-4111

Hawaii Dept. of Planning and
Econ. Devel.
Intl. Services Branch
P.O. Box 2359
Honolulu, HI   96806
(808) 548-3048

Econ. Devel. Corp. of Honolulu
1001 Bishop St.
Suite 855, Pacific Tower
Honolulu, HI   96813
(808) 545-4533

Foreign Trade Zone No. 9
Pier No. 2
Honolulu, HI   96813
(808) 548-5435

U.S. Dept. of Commerce (ITA)
P.O. Box 50026
Honolulu, HI   96850
(808) 546-8694

Idaho

Div. of Econ. & Community
Affairs
Statehouse, Rm. 108
Boise, ID   83720
(208) 334-3417

Intl. Trade Committee
Greater Boise Chamber of
Commerce
P.O. Box 2368
Boise, ID   83701
(208) 344-5515

Idaho World Trade Assn.
Box 660
Twin Falls, ID   83301
(208) 326-5116

District Export Council
Statehouse, Rm. 225
Boise, ID   83720
(208) 334-2200

Idaho Intl. Institute
1112 S. Owyhee
Boise, ID   83705

U.S. Dept. of Commerce (ITA)
Statehouse, Rm. 113
Boise, ID   83720
(208) 334-9254

Illinois

American Assn. of Exporters
and Importers
7763 S. Kedzie Ave.
Chicago, IL   60652
(312) 471-1958

Automotive Exporters Club
of Chicago
3205 S. Shields Ave.
Chicago, IL   60616
(312) 567-6500

Carnets
U.S. Council for Intl. Business
1900 E. Golf Rd., Suite 740
Schaumburg, IL   60195
(312) 490-9696

Central Illinois Coordinating
Committee for Intl. Trade
205 Arcade Bldg.
725 Wright St.
Champaign, IL   61820
(217) 333-1465

Chamber of Commerce of Upper
Rock Island County
622 19th St.
Moline, IL   61265
(309) 762-3661

Chicago Assn. of Commerce &
Industry
World Trade Div.
200 N. Lasalle
Chicago, IL   60603
(312) 580-6900

Chicago Convention and Tourism
Bureau, Inc.
McCormick Place-on-the-Lake
Chicago, IL   60616
(312) 225-5000

Chicago Econ. Devel.
Commission
Intl. Business Div.
20 N. Clark St., 28th Floor
Chicago, IL   60602
(312) 744-8666

Chicago Midwest Credit
Management Assn.
315 South NW. Hwy.
Park Ridge, IL   60068
(312) 696-3000

Chicago Regional Port District
12800 S. Butler at Lake Calumet
Chicago, IL   60633
(312) 646-4400

Customs Brokers and Foreign
Freight
Forwarders Assn. of Chicago,
Inc.
P.O. Box 66365
Chicago, IL   60666
(312) 992-4100

Foreign Credit Insurance Assn.
20 N. Clark St., Suite 910
Chicago, IL   60602
(312) 641-1915

Ill. Department of Agriculture
1010 Jorie Blvd.
Oak Brook, IL   60521
(312) 920-9256

Ill. Dept. of Commerce and
Community Affairs
Intl. Business Div.
310 S. Michigan Ave.
Suite 1000

Chicago, IL   60604
(312) 793-7164

Ill. District Export Council
55 E. Monroe, Rm. 1406
Chicago, IL   60603
(312) 353-4450

Ill. Manufacturers' Assn.
175 W. Jackson Blvd.
Suite 1321
Chicago, IL   60604
(312) 922-6575

Ill. State Chamber of Commerce
Intl. Trade Div.
20 N. Wacker Dr., Suite 1960
Chicago, IL   60606
(312) 372-7373

Intl. Business Council
MidAmerica (IBCM)
401 N. Wabash Ave., Suite 538
Chicago, IL   60611
(312) 222-1424

Mid-America International
Agri-Trade Council (MIATCO)
828 Davis St.
Evanston, IL   60201
(312) 368-4448

NW. Intl. Trade Club
P.O. Box 454
Elk Grove Village, IL   60007
(312) 793-2086

Overseas Sales & Marketing
Assn. of America, Inc.
3500 Devon Ave.
Lake Bluff, IL   60044
(312) 679-6070

Peoria Area Chamber of
Commerce
230 SW. Adams St.

Peoria, IL 61602
(309) 676-0755

U.S. Customs Service
55 E. Monroe, Suite 1501
Chicago, IL 60603
(312) 686-2143

U.S. Dept. of Commerce (ITA)
55 E. Monroe, Suite 1406
Chicago, IL 60603
(312) 353-4450

U.S. Small Business Admin.
Regional Export Devel.
219 S. Dearborn St., Suite 838
Chicago, IL 60604
(312) 886-0848

U.S. Great Lakes Shipping Assn.
3434 E. 95th St.
Chicago, IL 60617
(312) 978-0342

World Trade Club of N. Ill.
515 N. Court
Rockford, IL 61101
(815) 987-8100

Indiana

Forum for Intl. Professional
Services, Inc.
One Merchants Plaza
Suite 770S
Indianapolis, IN 46255
(317) 267-7309

Hudson Institute
620 Union Dr.
P.O. Box 648
Indianapolis, IN 46206
(317) 632-1787

Intl. Banking Committee
Indiana Bankers Assn.

1 N. Capitol, Suite 315
Indianapolis, IN 46204
(317) 632-9533

Intl. Center of Indianapolis
1050 W. 42nd St.
Indianapolis, IN 46208
(317) 923-1468

Intl. Devel. Group
Fort Wayne Chamber of Commerce
826 Ewing St.
Fort Wayne, IN 46802
(219) 424-1435

Intl. Law Section
Indiana State Bar Assn.
230 E. Ohio St.
Indianapolis, IN 46204
(317) 639-5465

Ind. Assn. of Credit Management
Intl. Credit Management
130 E. New York St.
Indianapolis, IN 46204
(317) 632-4444

Ind. Consortium for Intl.
Programs
N. Quad 240
Ball State University
Muncie, IN 47306
(317) 285-8780

Ind. Council on World Affairs
Inst. of Transnational Business
Ball State University
Muncie, IN 47306
(317) 285-5526

Ind. Dept. of Commerce
Agriculture Division
One N. Capitol, Suite 700
Indianapolis, IN 46204
(317) 232-8770

Ind. Dept. of Commerce
Intl. Trade Div.
Ind. Commerce Center, Suite 70
One N. Capitol
Indianapolis, IN 46204-2243
(317) 232-8845

Ind. Export Council
c/o U.S. Dept. of Commerce
Ind. Commerce Center, Suite 70
1 N. Capitol
Indianapolis, IN 46204
(317) 269-6214

Ind. Manufacturers Assn.
115 N. Pennsylvania St., Rm. 9
Indianapolis, IN 46204
(317) 632-2474

Ind. Port Commission Hdq.
143 W. Market St., Suite 204
Indianapolis, IN 46204
(317) 232-7150

Ind. State Chamber of Commerce
1 North Capitol, Suite 200
Indianapolis, IN 46204
(317) 634-6407

Indianapolis Airport Authority
Indianapolis Intl. Airport
P.O. Box 51605
Indianapolis, IN 46241
(317) 248-9594

Indianapolis Business
Devel. Fdn.
One Virginia Ave., 2nd Floor
Indianapolis, IN 46204
(317) 639-6131

Indianapolis Chamber of
Commerce
310 N. Meridian
Indianapolis, IN 46204
(317) 267-2900

Indianapolis Econ. Devel. Corp.
48 Monument Circle
Indianapolis, IN 46204
(317) 236-6262

Indianapolis Foreign Trade
Zone, Inc.
Park Fletcher Industrial
Research Center
5545 W. Minnesota St.
P.O. Box 51681
Indianapolis, IN 46251
(317) 247-1181

Michiana World Trade Club
401 E. Colfax, Suite 310
P.O. Box 1677
South Bend, IN 46634
(219) 234-0051

Southwind-Maritime Center
P.O. Box 529
Mount Vernon, IN 47620
(812) 838-4382

Tippecanoe World Trade Council
Greater Lafayette Chamber
of Commerce
P.O. Box 348
Lafayette, IN 47902
(317) 742-4041

Tri-State World Trade Council
329 Main St.
Evansville, IN 47708
(812) 425-8147

U.S. Customs Service
Indianapolis Airport
P.O. Box 51612
Indianapolis, IN 46251-0612
(317) 248-4060

U.S. Dept. of Commerce (ITA)
357 U.S. Courthouse
46 E. Ohio St.

Indianapolis, IN   46204
(317) 269-6214

U.S. Small Business Admin.
575 N. Pennsylvania, Rm. 578
Indianapolis, IN   46204
(317) 269-7272

World Trade Club of Ind., Inc.
P.O. Box 986
Indianapolis, IN   46206
(317) 285-5207

Iowa

Intl. Trade Bureau
P.O. Box 4860
Cedar Rapids, IA   52407
(319) 398-5310

Iowa Assn. of Business &
Industry
706 Employers Mutual Bldg.
Des Moines, IA   50309
(505) 281-3138

Iowa Devel. Commission
600 E. Court Ave., Suite A
Des Moines, IA   50309
(515) 281-3581

Iowa-Ill. Intl. Trade Assn.
Membership and Community
Relations
112 E. 3rd St.
Davenport, IA   52801
(319) 322-1706

Siouxland Intl. Trade Assn.
Legislative and Agriculture
Affairs
101 Pierce St.
Sioux City, IA   51101
(712) 255-7903

U.S. Dept. of Commerce (ITA)

817 Fed. Bldg.
210 Walnut St.
Des Moines, IA   50309
(515) 284-4222

Kansas

Intl. Trade Club of Greater
Kansas City
920 Main St., Suite 600
Kansas City, MO   64105
(816) 221-1460

Intl. Trade Institute
1627 Anderson
Manhattan, KS   66502
(913) 532-7699

Kans. Board of Agriculture
109 SW. 9th St.
Topeka, KS   66612
(913) 296-3736

Kans. Dept. of Econ. Devel.
Intl. Devel.
503 Kansas Ave., 6th Floor
Topeka, KS   66603
(913) 296-3483

Kansas-NW. Mo. District
Export Council
P.O. Box 626
Beliot, KS   67420
(913) 738-2261

U.S. Dept. of Commerce (ITA)
601 E. 12th St., Rm. 635
Kansas City, MO   64106
(816) 374-3141

U.S. Dept. of Commerce (ITA)
River Park Place, Suite 656
727 N. Waco
Wichita, KS   67203
(316) 269-6160

World Trade Council of Wichita
350 W. Douglas Ave.
Wichita, KS   67202
(316) 265-7771

Kentucky

Bluegrass Area Devel. District
3220 Nicholasvile Rd.
Lexington, KY   40503
(606) 272-6656

Ky. Commerce Cabinet
Office of Intl. Marketing
Capital Plaza Tower, 24th Fl.
Frankfort, KY   40601
(502) 564-2170

Ky. District Export Council
P.O. Box 33247
Louisville, KY   40232
(502) 966-0550

Kentuckiana World Commerce
Council
P.O. Box 58456
Louisville, KY   40258
(502) 583-5551

(City of) Louisville
609 W. Jefferson St.
Louisville, KY   40202
(502) 587-3051

N. Ky. Chamber of Commerce
1717 Dixie Hwy.
Covington, KY   41011
(606) 341-9500

TASKIT (Tech. Assistance to
Stimulating Ky. Intl. Trade)
College of Business and Econ.
University of Kentucky
Lexington, KY   40506-0205
(606) 257-7663

U.S. Dept. of Commerce (ITA)
U.S.P.O. & Courthouse Bldg.
601 W. Broadway, Rm. 636B
Louisville, KY   40202
(502) 582-5066

Louisiana

Chamber of Commerce/New
Orleans and River Region
301 Camp St.
New Orleans, LA   70130
(504) 527-6900

Intl. Trade Mart
Executive Offices, Suite 2900
2 Canal St.
New Orleans, LA   70130
(504) 529-1601

La. Dept. of Commerce
Office of Intl. Trade, Finance
and Devel.
P.O. Box 94185
Baton Rouge, LA   70804-9185
(504) 342-5362

Port of New Orleans
Trade Devel.
P.O. Box 60046
New Orleans, LA   70160
(504) 528-3259

U.S. Dept. of Commerce (ITA)
432 Intl. Trade Mart
2 Canal St.
New Orleans, LA   70130
(504) 589-6546

World Trade Club of Greater
New Orleans
1132 Intl. Trade Mart
2 Canal St.
New Orleans, LA   70130
(504) 525-7201

Maine

Maine State Devel. Office
State House, Station 59
Augusta, ME   04333
(207) 289-2656

Maine World Trade Assn.
1 Memorial Circle
Augusta, ME   04330
(207) 622-0234

U.S. Dept. of Commerce (ITA)
c/o Maine Devel. Fdn.
1 Memorial Circle
Augusta, ME   04330
(207) 622-8249

Maryland

Greater Balitmore Committee,
Inc.
Suite 900, 2 Hopkins Plaza
Baltimore, MD   21201
(301) 727-2820

Baltimore Econ. Devel. Corp.
36 S. Charles St., Suite 2400
Baltimore, MD   21201
(301) 837-9305

(The) Export Club
326 N. Charles St.
Baltimore, MD   21201
(301) 727-8831

Md. Dept. of Econ. and
Community Devel.
45 Calvert St.
Annapolis, MD   21401
(301) 269-3176

Md./Washington, D.C., Export
Council
415 U.S. Customhouse
Gay and Lombard Sts.
Baltimore, MD   21202
(301) 962-3560

Md. Port Administration
World Trade Center
Baltimore, MD   21202
(301) 659-4500

U.S. Dept. of Commerce (ITA)
Rm. 415, U.S. Customhouse
40 S. Gay St.
Baltimore, MD   21202
(301) 962-3560

U.S. Small Business Admin.
10 N. Calvert St.
Baltimore, MD   21202
(301) 962-2233

Massachusetts

Associated Industries of Mass.
462 Boylston St.
Boston, MA   02116
(617) 262-1180

Central Berkshire Chamber
of Commerce
Berkshire Common
Pittsfield, MA   01201
(413) 499-4000

Chamber of Commerce of
Attleboro Area
42 Union St.
Attleboro, MA   02703
(617) 222-0801

Commonwealth of Mass.
1 Ashburton Place
Boston, MA   02108
(617) 727-8380

Fall River Area Chamber of
Commerce
200 Pocasset St.
P.O. Box 1871
Fall River, MA   02722
(617) 676-8226

Foreign Trade Zone #28
Industrial Devel. Commission
1213 Purchase St.
New Bedford, MA   02740
(617) 997-6501

Greater Boston Chamber of
Commerce
125 High St.
Boston, MA   02110
(617) 426-1250

Greater Lawrence Chamber of
Commerce
300 Essex St.
Lawrence, MA   01840
(617) 687-9404

Greater Springfield Chamber
of Commerce
600 Bay State W. Plaza
Suite 600
1500 Main St.
Springfield, MA   01115
(413) 734-5671

Intl. Business Center of New
England, Inc.
22 Batterymarch St.
Boston, MA   02109
(617) 542-0426

Mass. Commission on Intl.
Trade & Foreign Investment
Suite 413F, State House
Boston, MA   02133
(617) 722-1673

Mass. Dept. of Commerce &
Devel.
100 Cambridge St.
Boston, MA   02202
(517) 727-3218

Mass. Dept. of Food &
Agriculture
100 Cambridge St.
Boston, MA   02202
(617) 727-3108

Massport
99 High St.
Boston, MA   02110
(617) 482-2930

National Marine Fisheries Ser.
14 Elm St.
Gloucester, MA   01930
(617) 281-3600

New Bedford Area Chamber of
Commerce
Rm. 407, First National Bank
Bldg.
New Bedford, MA   02742
(617) 999-5231

New England Council, Inc.
1020 Statler Bldg.
Boston, MA   02116
(617) 542-2580

New England Governors'
Conference, Inc.
76 Summer St.
Boston, MA   02110
(617) 423-6900

N. Suburban Chamber of Commerce
25-B Montvale Ave.
Woburn, MA   01801
(617) 933-3499

Smaller Business Assn. of New
England, Inc.
69 Hickory Drive
Waltham, MA   02154
(617) 890-9070

S. Middlesex Area Chamber of
Commerce
615 Concord St.
Framingham, MA   01701
(617) 879-5600

S. Shore Chamber of Commerce,
Inc.
36 Miller Stile Rd.
Quincy, MA   02169
(617) 479-1111

U.S. Dept. of Commerce (ITA)
441 Stuart St.
Boston, MA   02116
(617) 223-2312

U.S. Small Business Admin.
60 Batterymarch St.
Boston, MA   02110
(617) 223-3891

Waltham/West Suburban Chamber
of Commerce
663 Main St.
Waltham, MA   02154
(617) 894-4700

Watertown Chamber of Commerce
75 Main St.
Watertown, MA   02172
(617) 926-1017

Worcester Chamber of Commerce
Mechanics Tower, Suite 350
100 Front St.
Worcester, MA   01608
(617) 753-2924

Michigan

Adcraft Club of Detroit
2630 Book Bldg.
Detroit, MI   48226
(313) 962-7225

Ann Arbor Chamber of Commerce
207 E. Washington
Ann Arbor, MI   48104
(313) 665-4433

BC/CAL/KAL Port of Battle Creek
Foreign Trade Zone #43
P.O. Box 1438
Battle Creek, MI   49016
(616) 968-8197

City of Detroit
Community & Econ. Devel. Dept.
150 Michigan Ave. 7th Floor
Detroit, MI   48226
(313) 224-6533

Detroit Customhouse Brokers &
Foreign Freight Forwarders
Assn., Inc.
155 W. Congress, Rm. 420
Detroit, MI   48226
(313) 962-4681

Detroit/Wayne County Port Auth.
100 Renaissance Center
Suite 1370
Detroit, MI   48243
(313) 259-8077

Downriver Community Conference
15100 Northline
Southgate, MI   48195
(313) 283-8933

Flint Area Chamber of Commerce
708 Root, Rm. 123
Flint, MI   48503
(313) 232-7101

Greater Port Huron-Marysville
Chamber of Commerce
920 Pine Grove Ave.
Port Huron, MI   48060
(313) 985-7101

Greater Saginaw Chamber of
Commerce
901 S. Washington
Saginaw, MI   48606
(517) 752-7161

Great Lakes Trade Adjustment
Assistance Center
Institute of Science and Tech.
University of Michigan
2901 Baxter Rd.
Ann Arbor, MI   48109
(313) 763-4085

Greater Detroit Chamber of
Commerce
150 Michigan Ave.
Detroit, MI   48226
(313) 964-4000

Greater Grand Rapids Chamber
of Commerce
17 Fountain St., NW.
Grand Rapids, MI   49502
(616) 459-7221

Kalamazoo Chamber of Commerce
P.O. Box 1169
Kalamazoo, MI   49007
(616) 381-4000

Macomb County Chamber of
Commerce
10 North Ave.
Mt. Clemens, MI   48043
(313) 463-1528

Mich. Bankers Assn.
6105 W. St. Joseph Hwy.
Lansing, MI   48917
(517) 321-1600

Mich. Dept. of Agriculture
P.O. Box 30017
Lansing, MI   48909
(517) 373-1054

Mich. Dept. of Commerce
Office of Intl. Devel.
P.O. Box 30105
Lansing, MI   48909
(517) 373-6390

Mich. District Export Council
445 Fed. Bldg.
Detroit, MI   48226
(313) 226-3650

Mich. Manufacturers Assn.
124 E. Kalamazoo
Lansing, MI   48933
(517) 372-5900

Mich. State Chamber of
Commerce
200 N. Washington Sq.
Suite 400
Lansing, MI   48933
(517) 371-2100

Motor Vehicle Manufacturers
Assn. of USA
300 New Center Bldg.
Detroit, MI   48202
(313) 872-4311

Muskegon Area Chamber of
Commerce
1065 4th St.
Muskegon, MI   49441
(616) 722-3751

Technology Intl. Council
207 E. Washington St.
Ann Arbor, MI   48104
(313) 665-4433

Twin Cities Area Chamber of
Commerce
P.O. Box 1208
685 W. Main St.
Benton Harbor, MI   49022
(616) 925-0044

U.S. Customs Service
2nd Fl., Patrick V. McNamara
Bldg.
Detroit, MI 48226
(313) 226-3177

U.S. Dept. of Commerce (ITA)
445 Fed. Bldg.
Detroit, MI 48226
(313) 226-3650

U.S. Small Business Admin.
515 Patrick V. McNamara Bldg.
Detroit, MI 48226
(313) 226-7240

W. Mich. World Trade Club
P.O. Box 2242
Grand Rapids, MI   49501
(616) 456-9622

World Trade Club of Detroit
150 Michigan Ave.
Detroit, MI 48226
(313) 964-4000

Minnesota

Minn. Export Finance Auth.
90 W. Plato Blvd.
St. Paul, MN 55107
(612) 297-4659

Minn. Trade Office
90 W. Plato Blvd.
St. Paul, MN 55107
(612) 297-4655

Minn. World Trade Assn.
33 E. Wentworth Ave., 101
West St. Paul, MN 55118
(612) 457-1038

Minn. World Trade Center
1300 Conwed Tower

444 Cedar St.
St. Paul, MN 55101
(612) 297-1580

Seaway Port Authority of
Duluth
P.O. Box 6877
Duluth, MN 55806
(218) 727-8525

U.S. Dept. of Commerce (ITA)
108 Fed. Bldg.
110 S. 4th St.
Minneapolis, MN 55401
(612) 349-3338

Mississippi

Greenville Port Commission
P.O. Box 446
Greenville, MS   38701
(601) 335-2683

Intl. Trade Club of Miss. Inc.
P.O. Box 16353
Jackson, MS 39236
(601) 956-1715

Jackson County Port Auth.
P.O. Box 70
Pascagoula, MS 39567
(601) 762-4041

Miss. Dept. of Econ. Devel.
Marketing Division
P.O. Box 849
Jackson, MS 39205
(601) 359-3444

Miss. State Port Auth. at
Gulfport
P.O. Box 40
Gulfport, MS 39502
(601) 865-4306

U.S. Dept. of Commerce (ITA)
328 Jackson Mall Ofc. Center
300 Woodrow Wilson Blvd.
Jackson, MS 39213
(601) 960-4388

Missouri

Intl. Trade Club of Greater
Kansas City
920 Main St., Suite 600
Kansas City, MO 64105
(816) 221-1460

Grater Ozarks Intl. Trade Club
P.O. Box 1687
Springfield, MO 65805
(417) 862-5567

Mo. Dept. of Agriculture
Intl. Marketing Division
P.O. Box 630
Jefferson City, MO 65102
(314) 751-5611

Mo. Dept. of Commerce
Intl. Business Office
P.O. Box 118
Jefferson City, MO 65102
(314) 751-4855

Mo. District Export Council
120 S. Central, Suite 400
St. Louis, MO 63105
(314) 425-3302

U.S. Dept. of Commerce (ITA)
601 E. 12th St.
Kansas City, MO 64106
(816) 374-3142

U.S. Dept. of Commerce (ITA)
120 S. Central, Suite 400
St. Louis, MO 63105
(314) 425-3301

World Trade Club of St.
Louis, Inc.
111 N. Taylor Ave.
Kirkwood, MO 63122
(314) 965-9940

Montana

49th Parallel Institute
Dept. of Political Science
Montana State University
Bozeman, MT 59717
(406) 994-6690

Montana Dept. of Commerce
Business Assistance Div.
1424-9th Ave.
Helena, MT 59620
(406) 444-3923

U.S. Dept. of Commerce (ITA)
721 19th St., Rm. 113
Denver, CO 80202
(303) 844-2900

Nebraska

Midwest Intl. Trade Assn.
c/o NBC, 13th & O Sts.
Lincoln, NE 68108
(402) 472-4321

Nebraska Dept. of Econ. Devel.
State Devel. and Intl. Div.
301 Centennial Mall S.
Lincoln, NE 68509
(402) 471-4670

Omaha Chamber of Commerce
1301 Harney St.
Omaha, NE 68102
(402) 346-5000

U.S. Dept. of Commerce (ITA)
300 S. 19th St.
Omaha, NE 68102
(402) 221-3664

U.S. Small Business Admin.
300 S. 19th St., 2nd Floor
Omaha, NE 68102
(402) 221-3607

Nevada

Commission on Econ. Devel.
600 E. Williams, Suite 203
Carson City, NV 89710
(702) 885-4325

Econ. Devel. Auth. of W. Nev.
P.O. Box 11710
Reno, NV 89510
(702) 322-4004

Latin Chamber of Commerce
P.O. Box 7534
Las Vegas, NV 89125-2534
(702) 385-7367

Nev. Devel. Auth.
P.O. Box 11128
Las Vegas, NV 89111
(702) 739-8222

Nev. District Export Council
P.O. Box 11007
Reno, NV 89520
(702) 784-3401

U.S. Dept. of Commerce (ITA)
1755 E. Plumb Lane, Suite 152
Reno, NV 89502
(702) 784-5203

New Hampshire

(State of) New Hampshire
Dept. of Resources and Econ.
Devel.
P.O. Box 856
Concord, NH 03301
(603) 271-2341

S. N.H. Assn. of Commerce and
Industry
4 Manchester St.
P.O. Box 1123
Nashua, NH 03601
(603) 882-8106

U.S. Dept. of Commerce (ITA)
441 Stuart St.
Boston, MA 02116
(617) 223-2312

New Jersey

Delaware River Port Auth.
World Trade Div.
Bridge Plaza
Camden, NJ 08101
(609) 963-6420, ext. 264

Intl. Business Council
240 W. State St., Suite 1412
Trenton, NJ 08608

Intl. Round Table
Bergen County Community
College
400 Paramus Rd.
Paramus, NJ 07652
(201) 477-7167

(State of) N.J. Div. of Intl.
Trade
744 Broad St., Rm. 1709
Newark, NJ 07102
(201) 648-3518

N.J./N.Y. Port Auth.
One World Trade Center, 63-S
New York, NY 10048
(212) 466-8499

Rutgers Small Business Devel.
Center
180 University Ave.
Newark, NJ 07102
(201) 648-5950

Union County Chamber of
Commerce
Intl. Trade Committee
135 Jefferson Ave.
P.O. Box 300
Elizabeth, NJ   07207
(201) 352-0900

U.S. Assn. of Credit and
Finance Execs.
Foreign Credit Div.
P.O. Box 130
405 Washington Ave.
Kenilworth, NJ   07033
(201) 272-9191

U.S. Dept. of Commerce (ITA)
Capital Plaza, 8th Floor
240 W. State St.
Trenton, NJ   08608
(609) 989-2100

World Trade Assn. of N.J.
5 Commerce St.
Newark, NJ   07102
(201) 623-7070

New Mexico

Econ. Devel. and Tourism Dept.
Intl. Division
Bataan Memorial Bldg.
Santa Fe, NM   87503
(505) 827-3145

Foreign Trade Zone, N.M.
P.O. Box 26928
Albuquerque, NM   87125
(505) 842-0088

N.M. Dept. of Agriculture
P.O. Box 5600
Las Cruces, NM   88003
(505) 646-4929

N.M. Foreign Trade &
Investment Council, Inc.
Mail Stop 150, Alvarado Sq.
Albuquerque, NM   87158
(505) 848-4632

N.M. Industry Devel. Corp.
300 San Mateo NE., Suite 815
Albuquerque, NM   87118

U.S. Dept. of Commerce (ITA)
517 Gold SW.
Albuquerque, NM   87102
(505) 766-2386

New York

Albany-Colonie Regional
Chamber of Commerce
14 Corporate Woods Blvd.
Albany, NY   12211
(518) 434-1214

American Assn. of Exporters
and Importers
11 W. 42nd St.
New York, NY   10036
(212) 944-2230

American Management Assns.
135 W. 50th St.
New York, NY   10020
(212) 586-8100

Buffalo Area Chamber of
Commerce
107 Delaware Ave.
Buffalo, NY   14202
(716) 849-6682

Buffalo World Trade Assn.
538 Ellicott Sq. Bldg.
Buffalo, NY   14203
(716) 854-1019

Foreign Credit Insurance Assn.
40 Rector St., 11th Floor
New York, NY 10006

Intl. Bus. Council of Rochester
Area Chamber of Commerce
Intl. Trade & Transportation
55 St. Paul St.
Rochester, NY 14604
(716) 454-2220

Intl. Trade Council, Greater
Syracuse Chamber of Commerce
100 E. Onondaga St.
Syracuse, NY 13202
(315) 470-1343

Intl. Executives Assn., Inc.
114 E. 32nd St., Suite 1301
New York, NY 10016
(212) 683-9755

Long Island Assn. Inc.
80 Hauppage Rd.
Commack, NY 11725
(516) 499-4400

Mohawk Valley World Trade
Council
P.O. Box 4126
Utica, NY 13540
(315) 797-1630

Nat. Assn. of Credit Managers
(NACM)
Foreign Credit Insurance Bureau
(FCIB)
475 Park Ave. S.
New York, NY 10016
(212) 578-4710

Nat. Assn. of Credit Managers
(NACB)
Upstate New York
250 Delaware Ave.
Buffalo, NY 14202
(716) 845-7018

Nat. Assn. of Export Cos. Inc.
396 Broadway, Suite 603
New York, NY 10013
(212) 966-2271

Nat. Customs Brokers &
Forwarders Assn. of America,
Inc.
One World Trade Center
  Rm. 1109
New York, NY 10048
(212) 432-0050

N.Y. Chamber of Commerce &
Industry
200 Madison Ave.
New York, NY 10016
(212) 561-2028

N.Y. State Dept. of Commerce
Div. of Intl. Commerce
230 Park Ave.
New York, NY 10169
(212) 309-0500

Overseas Automotive Club, Inc.
222 Cedar Lane
Teaneck, NJ 07666
(212) 836-6999

Port Auth. of N.Y. and N.J.
Trade Devel. Office
Rm. 64-E
One World Trade Center
New York, NY 10048
(212) 466-8333

Rochester Area Chamber of
Commerce
World Trade Dept.
Intl. Trade & Transportation
55 St. Paul St.
Rochester, NY 14604
(716) 454-2220

Tappan Zee Intl. Trade Assn.
One Blue Hill Plaza
Pearl River, NY   10965
(914) 735-7040

U.S. Council for Intl. Business
1212 Ave. of the Americas
New York, NY   10036
(212) 354-4480

U.S. Dept. of Commerce (ITA)
1312 Fed. Bldg.
Buffalo, NY   14202
(716) 846-4191

U.S. Dept. of Commerce (ITA)
26 Fed. Plaza, Rm. 3718
New York, NY   10278
(212) 264-0634

U.S. Dept. of Commerce (ITA)
121 E. Ave.
Rochester, NY   14604
(716) 263-6480

U.S. Small Business Admin.
26 Fed. Plaza, Rm. 3130
New York, NY   10278
(212) 264-4507

U.S. Small Business Admin.
100 S. Clinton St.
Syracuse, NY   13260
(315) 423-5383

Westchester County Assn., Inc.
World Trade Club of
Westchester
235 Mamaroneck Ave.
White Plains, NY   10605
(914) 948-6444

World Commerce Assn. of
Central N.Y.
100 E. Onandaga St.
Syracuse, NY   13202
(315) 470-1343

World Trade Club of Long
Island
c/o LIREX, 1425 Old Country Rd.
Plainview, L.I., NY   11803

World Trade Club of N.Y., Inc.
396 Broadway, Suite 603
New York, NY   10013
(212) 966-2271

World Trade Institute
One World Trade Center
New York, NY   10048
(212) 466-4044

North Carolina

N.C. Dept. of Agriculture
P.O. Box 27647
Raleigh, NC   27611
(919) 733-7912

N.C. Dept. of Commerce
Intl. Div.
430 N. Salisbury St.
Raleigh, NC   27611
(919) 733-7193

N.C. District Export Council
P.O. Box 12057
Res. Triangle Park, NC   27709
(919) 787-2530

N.C. State University
Intl. Trade Center
P.O. Box 5125
Raleigh, NC   27650
(919) 737-7912

N.C. World Trade Assn.
P.O. Box 327
Wilmington, NC   28402
(919) 763-9841

U.S. Dept. of Commerce (ITA)
P.O. Box 1950
Greensboro, NC   27402
(919) 378-5345

North Dakota

Fargo Chamber of Commerce
321 N. 4th St.
Fargo, NC   58108
(701) 237-5678

N.D. Econ. Devel. Commission
Industrial Devel. and Intl. Div.
Liberty Memorial Bldg.
State Capital Grounds
Bismarck, ND   58505
(701) 224-2810

U.S. Dept. of Commerce (ITA)
300 S. 19th St.
Omaha, NE   68102
(402) 221-3664

U.S. Small Business Admin.
P.O. Fed. Bldg.
Fargo, ND   58108
(701) 237-5771, ext. 131

Ohio

Cincinnati Council on World
Affairs
1028 Dixie Terminal Bldg.
Cincinnati, OH   45202
(513) 621-2320

Cleveland Council on World
Affairs
601 Rockwell Ave.
Cleveland, OH   44114
(216) 781-3730

Cleveland World Trade Assn.
690 Huntington Bldg.
Cleveland, OH   44115
(216) 621-3300

Columbus Area Chamber of
Commerce
World Trade
37 N. High St.
Columbus, OH   43216
(614) 221-1321

Columbus Council on World
Affairs
57 Jefferson Ave.
Columbus, OH   43215
(614) 461-0632

Commerce & Industry Assn. of
Greater Elyria
P.O. Box 179
Elyria, OH   44036
(216) 322-5438

Dayton Council on World
Affairs
300 College Park
Dayton, OH   45469
(513) 229-2319

Dayton Devel. Council
1980 Kettering Tower
Dayton, OH   45423-1980
(513) 226-8222

Greater Cincinnati Chamber of
Commerce
120 W. 5th St.
Cincinnati, OH   45202
(513) 579-3143

Greater Cincinnati World Trade
Assn.
120 W. 5th St.
Cincinnati, OH   45202
(513) 579-3122

Intl. Business and Trade Assn.
of Akron
Regional Development Board
One Cascade Plaza, Suite 800
Akron, OH 44308
(216) 379-3157

International Trade Institute
5055 N. Main St.
Dayton, OH 45415
(513) 276-5995

N. Central Ohio Intl. Trade
Club
Mansfield Richland Area
Chamber of Commerce
55 N. Mulberry St.
Mansfield, OH 44902
(419) 522-3211

N. Ohio District Export Council
Plaza Nine Bldg.
55 Erieview Plaza, Suite 700
Cleveland, OH 44114
(216) 522-4750

Ohio Dept. of Agriculture
Ohio Dept. Bldg., Rm. 607
65 S. Front St.
Columbus, OH 43215
(614) 466-4104

Ohio Dept. of Devel.
Intl. Trade Div.
30 E. Broad St.
Columbus, OH 43216
(614) 466-5017

Ohio Foreign Commerce Assn.,
Inc.
1111 Chester Ave., Rm. 506A
Cleveland, OH 44114
(216) 696-7000

Port of Cleveland

Cleveland-Cuyahoga County Port
Auth.
101 Erieside Ave.
Cleveland, OH 44114-1095
(216) 241-8004

Port of Toledo
Toledo-Lucas County Port Auth.
One Maritime Plaza
Toledo, OH 43604-1866
(419) 243-8251

S. Ohio District Export Council
9504 Fed. Bldg.
550 Main St.
Cincinnati, OH 45202
(513) 684-2944

Toledo Area Intl. Trade Assn.
218 Huron St.
Toledo, OH 43604
(419) 243-8191

U.S. Customs Service
55 Erieview Plaza
Cleveland, OH 44114
(216) 522-4284

U.S. Dept. of Commerce (ITA)
9504 Fed. Bldg.
550 Main St.
Cincinnati, OH 45202
(513) 684-2944

U.S. Dept. of Commerce (ITA)
Plaza Nine Bldg.
55 Erieview Plaza, Suite 700
Cleveland, OH 44114
(216) 522-4750

U.S. Small Business Admin.
317 AJC Fed. Bldg.
1240 E. 9th St.
Cleveland, OH 44199
(216) 522-4194

World Trade Committee of
Youngstown
Area Chamber of Commerce
200 Wick Bldg.
Youngstown, OH   44503-1474
(216) 744-2131

World Trade Eucation Center
Cleveland State University
University Ctr. Bldg., Rm. 460
Cleveland, OH   44115
(216) 687-3733

World Trade & Technology Ctr.
10793 State Rte. 37 W.
Sunbury, OH   43074
(614) 965-2974

Oklahoma

Foreign Trade Zone #53
Tulsa Port of Catoosa
5555 Bird Creek Ave.
Catoosa, OK   74015
(918) 266-5830

Foreign Trade Zone #106
One Santa Fe Plaza
Oklahoma City, OK   73102
(405) 278-8900

Metropolitan Tulsa Chamber of
Commerce
Econ. Devel. Div.
616 S. Boston Ave.
Tulsa, OK   74119
(918) 585-1201

Muskogee City-County Port Auth.
Rte. 6, Port 50
Muskogee, OK   74401
(918) 682-7886

Oklahoma City Chamber of
Commerce
Econ. and Community Devel.
One Santa Fe Plaza

Oklahoma City, OK   73102
(405) 278-8900

Oklahoma City Intl. Trade
Assn.
P.O. Box 66
Perry, OK   73077
(405) 336-4402

Okla. Dept. of Econ. Devel.
Intl. Division
4024 Lincoln Blvd.
Oklahoma City, OK   73105
(405) 521-2401

Okla. District Export Council
4024 Lincoln Blvd.
Oklahoma City, OK   73105
(405) 231-5302

Okla. State Chamber of
Commerce
4020 Lincoln Blvd.
Oklahoma City, OK   73105
(405) 424-4003

Okla. State Dept. of
Agriculture
2800 Lincoln Blvd.
Oklahoma City, OK   73105
(405) 521-3864

Tulsa Port of Catoosa
5350 Cimarron Rd.
Catoosa, OK   74015
(918) 266-2291

Tulsa World Trade Assn.
1821 N. 106th E. Ave.
Tulsa, OK   74116
(918) 836-0338

U.S. Dept. of Commerce (ITA)
4024 Lincoln Blvd.
Oklahoma City, OK   73105
(405) 231-5302

Oregon

Eugene Area Chamber of Commerce
1401 Willamette
P.O. Box 1107
Eugene, OR   97440
(503) 484-1314

Institute for Intl. Trade and
Commerce
Portland State University
1912 S.W. Sixth Ave., Rm. 260
Portland, OR   97207
(503) 229-3246

Oregon District Export Council
1220 SW. 3rd Ave., Rm. 618
Portland, OR   97209
(503) 292-9219

Oregon Econ. Devel. Dept.
Business Information Div.
595 Cottage St., NE.
Salem, OR   97310
(503) 373-1231

Pacific Northwest Intl. Trade
Assn.
200 SW. Market
Suite 220
Portland, OR   97201
(503) 228-4361

U.S. Dept. of Commerce (ITA)
1220 SW. 3rd Ave., Rm. 618
Portland, OR   97209
(503) 221-3001

Western Wood Products Assn.
Yeon Bldg.
Portland, OR   97204
(503) 224-3930

Pennsylvania

American Society of Intl.
Executives, Inc.
Dublin Hall, Suite 419
Blue Bell, PA   19422
(215) 643-3040

Assessment of Intl. Markets
Program
382 Mervis Hall
University of Pittsburgh
Pittsburgh, PA   15260
(412) 624-1777

Del. River Port Authority
Bridge Plaza
Camden, NJ   08101
(215) 925-8780

Foreign Trade Zone #33
Reg. Industrial Devel. Corp.
Union Trust Bldg.
Pittsburgh, PA   15219
(412) 471-3939

Intl. Business Forum
42 S. 15th St., Suite 315
Philadelphia, PA   19102
(215) 568-2710

Intl. Trade Devel. Assn.
P.O. Box 279
Chalfont, PA   18914
(215) 822-6893

Intl. Trade Executives
Club of Erie
c/o Manufacturers Assn. of Erie
33 E. 8th St.
Erie, PA   16507
(814) 459-3335

Intl. Trade Executives Club of
Pittsburgh
2002 Fed. Bldg.
1000 Liberty Ave.
Pittsburgh, PA   15222
(412) 644-2850

(215) 928-9100

N. Central Pa. Regional
Planning and Devel. Commission
651 Montmorenci Ave.
Ridgeway, PA   15853
(814) 773-3162

NW. Pa. Regional Planning and
Devel. Commission
Biery Bldg., Suite 406
Franklin, PA   16323
(814) 437-3024

Pa. Dept. of Agriculture
Bureau of Agricultural Devel.
2301 N. Cameron St.
Harrisburg, PA   17110
(717) 783-8460

Pa. Dept. of Commerce
Bureau of Domestic and Intl.
Commerce
453 Forum Bldg.
Harrisburg, PA   17120
(717) 787-7190

(City of) Philadelphia
Municipal Services Bldg.
Rm. 1660
Philadelphia, PA   19102
(215) 686-3647

(Greater) Philadelphia
Chamber of Commerce
1346 Chestnut St., Suite 800
Philadelphia, PA   19107
(215) 545-1234

Philadelphia Export Network
3508 Market St., Suite 100
Philadelphia, PA   19104
(215) 898-4189

Philadelphia Port Corp.
6th & Chestnut St.
Philadelphia, PA   19106

Pittsburgh Consular Assn.
Consul de Mexico, Suite 3201
4297 Greensburg Pike
Pittsburgh, PA   15221
(412) 271-5900

Pittsburgh Council for Intl.
Visitors
139 University Place
Pittsburgh, PA   15260
(412) 624-7929

Port Auth. of Allegheny County
514 Wood St.
Pittsburgh, PA   15222
(412) 237-7460

Port of Erie-West
507 Municipal Bldg.
Erie, PA   16501
(814) 456-8561

Reading Foreign Trade Assn.
35 N. 6th St.
Reading, PA   19603
(215) 320-2976

S. Alleghenies Regional
Planning and Devel. Commission
S. Alleghenies Plaza, Suite 100
1506 11th Ave.
Altoona, PA   16601
(814) 946-1641

SW. Pa. Econ. Devel. District
355 5th Ave., Room 141
Pittsburgh, PA   15222
(412) 391-1240

Trade Adjustment Assistance
Center
One E. Penn. Sq., Suite 14
Philadelphia, PA   19107
(215) 568-7740

Trade Adjustment Assistance
Center
Investment Bldg., Rm. 1001
239 4th Ave.
Pittsburgh, PA   15222
(412) 566-1732

U.S. Customs Service
822 Fed. Bldg.
1000 Liberty Ave.
Pittsburgh, PA   15232
(412) 644-3589

U.S. Dept. of Commerce (ITA)
Erie Associate Office
c/o Manufacturers Assn. of Erie
33 E. 8th St.
Erie, PA   16507
(814) 459-3335

U.S. Dept. of Commerce (ITA)
9448 Fed. Bldg.
600 Arch St.
Philadelphia, PA   19106
(215) 597-2866

U.S. Dept. of Commerce (ITA)
2002 Fed. Bldg.
1000 Liberty Ave.
Pittsburgh, PA   15222
(412) 644-2850

U.S. Small Business Admin.
One Bala Plaza, Suite 400 E.
Lobby
Bala Cynwyd, PA   19004
(215) 596-5801 .

U.S. Small Business Admin.
Convention Tower, 5th Floor
960 Penn Ave.
Pittsburgh, PA   15222
(412) 644-5438

W. Pa. District Export Council

1000 Liberty Ave., Rm. 2002
Pittsburgh, PA   15222
(412) 644-2850

Women's Intl. Trade Assn.
P.O. Box 40004, Continental
Station
Philadelphia, PA   19106
(215) 923-6900

World Trade Assn. of
Philadelphia, Inc.
820 Land Title Bldg.
Philadelphia, PA   19110
(215) 563-8887

Puerto Rico

District Export Council
252 Tetuan St.
San Juan, PR   00901
(809) 721-7600

P.R. Chamber of Commerce
P.O. Box 3789
San Juan, PR   00904
(809) 721-6060

P.R. Dept. of Commerce
P.O. Box 4275
San Juan, PR   00905
(809) 721-3290

P.R. Econ. Devel. Admin.
GPO Box 2350
San Juan, PA   00936
(809) 758-4747

P.R. Manufacturers Assn.
P.O. Box 2410
Hato Rey, PR   00919
(809) 759-9445

P.R. Products Assn.
GPO Box 3631
San Juan, PR   00936
(809) 753-8484

U.S. Dept. of Commerce (ITA)
Rm. 659, Fed. Bldg.
Hato Rey, PR 00918
(809) 753-4555

Rhode Island

(Greater) Providence Chamber
of Commerce
10 Dorrance St.
Providence, RI   02903
(401) 521-5000

R.I. Dept. of Econ. Devel.
7 Jackson Walkway
Providence, RI   02903
(401) 277-2601

U.S. Dept. of Commerce (ITA)
c/o R.I. Dept. of Econ. Devel.
7 Jackson Walkway
Providence, RI   02903
(401) 277-2601

South Carolina

Governor's Export Advisory
Committee
Rt. 1, Box 501
Spartanburg, SC   29302
(803) 579-3050

Low County Intl. Trade Club
(Charleston)
P.O. Box 159
Charleston, SC   29402
(803) 571-0510

Midlands Trade Club (Columbia)
Rt. 2, Box 50A
Elgin, SC   29045
(803) 254-1237

Pee Dee Intl. Trade Club
(Florence)

P.O. Box 716
Kingstree, SC   29556
(803) 382-9393

S.C. State Devel. Board
P.O. Box 927
Columbia, SC   29202
(803) 758-2384

S.C. District Export Council
Strom Thurmond Fed. Bldg.
Suite 172
1835 Assembly St.
Columbia, SC   29201
(803) 765-5345

S.C. State Port Auth.
P.O. Box 817
Charleston, SC   29402
(803) 577-8100

W. S.C. Intl. Trade Club
(Greenville)
P.O. Box 8764
Greenville, SC   29604-8764
(803) 232-1045

U.S. Dept. of Commerce (ITA)
Strom Thurmond Fed. Bldg.
Suite 172
1835 Assembly St.
Columbia, SC   29201
(803) 765-5345

South Dakota

Rapid City Area Chamber of
Commerce
P.O. Box 747
Rapid City, SD   57709
(605) 343-1744

Sioux Falls Chamber of
Commerce
127 E. 10th St.
Sioux Falls, SD   57101
(605) 336-1620

S.D. Dept. of State Devel.
Capitol Lake Plaza
Pierre, SD   57501
(605) 773-5032

U.S. Dept. of Commerce (ITA)
300 S. 19th St.
Omaha, NE   68102
(402) 221-3664

U.S. Small Business Admin.
101 S. Main Ave.
Sioux Falls, SD   57102
(605) 336-2980, ext. 231

Tennessee

Chattanooga World Trade Council
1001 Market St.
Chattanooga, TN   37402

E. Tenn. Intl. Trade Club
P.O. Box 280
Knoxville, TN   37901
(615) 971-2027

Memphis World Trade Club
P.O. Box 3577
Memphis, TN   38103
(901) 320-2210

Mid-South Exporters Roundtable
P.O. Box 3521
Memphis, TN   38173
(901) 320-5811

Middle Tenn. World Trade Club
1101 Kermit Dr., Suite 112
Nashville, TN   37217

Tenn. Dept. of Agriculture
Ellington Agricultural Center

P.O. Box 40627, Melrose Station
Nashville, TN   37204
(615) 360-0103

Tenn. Dept. of Econ. and
Community Devel.
320 6th Ave., 7th Floor
Nashville, TN   37219-5308
(615) 741-4815

Tenn. District Export Council
3074 Sidco Dr.
Nashville, TN   37210
(615) 259-9300

U.S. Dept. of Commerce (ITA)
One Commerce Plaza, Suite 1427
Nashville, TN   37239
(615) 251-5161

Texas

Amarillo Chamber of Commerce
Amarillo Bldg.
301 S. Polk
Amarillo, TX   79101
(806) 374-5238

Brownsville Navigation
District of Cameron County
P.O. Box 3070
Brownsville, TX   78520
(512) 831-4592

Center for Intl. Business
World Trade Center, Suite 184
P.O. Box 58428
Dallas, TX   75258
(214) 742-7301

Dallas Chamber of Commerce
1507 Pacific
Dallas, TX   75201
(214) 954-1111

Dallas Council on World
Affairs
Fred Lange Center
1310 Annex, Suite 101
Dallas, TX   75204
(214) 827-7960

El Paso Chamber of Commerce
10 Civic Center Plaza
El Paso, TX 79944
(915) 544-7880

Foreign Credit Insurance Assn.
600 Travis, Suite 2860
Houston, TX 77002
(713) 227-0987

Ft. Worth Chamber of Commerce
700 Throckmorton
Fort Worth, TX   76102
(817) 336-2491

Houston Chamber of Commerce
1100 Milan Bldg., 25th Floor
Houston, TX 77002
(713) 651-1313

Houston District Export Council
6101 W. View Drive
Houston, TX 77055
(713) 686-4331

Houston Port Authority
1519 Capitol Ave., Box 2562
Houston, TX 77001
(713) 225-0671

Houston World Trade Assn.
1520 Texas Ave., Suite 239
Houston, TX 77002
(713) 225-0967

Lubbock Chamber of Commerce
14th St. & Ave. K
P.O. Box 561

Lubbock, TX 79408
(806) 763-4666

N. Dallas Chamber of Commerce
10707 Preston Rd.
Dallas, TX 75230
(214) 368-6653

N. Tex. Commission
P.O. Box 61246
DFW Airport, TX 75261
(214) 574-4430

N. Tex. Customs Brokers &
Foreign Freight Forwarders
Assn.
P.O. Box 225464
DFW Airport, TX 75261
(214) 456-0730

N. Tex. Dist. Export Council
4448 Willow Lane
Dallas, TX 75234
(214) 788-1340

Odessa Chamber of Commerce
P.O. Box 3626
Odessa, TX 79760
(915) 332-9111

Port of Beaumont
P.O. Drawer 2297
Beaumont, TX 77704
(713) 835-5367

Port of Corpus Christi
P.O. Box 1541
Corpus Christi, TX 78403
(512) 882-5633

Port of Port Arthur
Box 1428
Port Authur, TX 77640
(713) 983-2011

(Greater) San Antonio Chamber
of Commerce
P.O. Box 1628
San Antonio, TX   78296
(512) 227-8181

Texas City Terminal Railway
Co. (Port)
P.O. Box 591
Texas City, TX   77590
(713) 945-4461

Tex. Dept. of Agriculture
Export Services Div.
P.O. Box 12847, Capitol Station
Austin, TX   78711
(512) 475-2760

Tex. Econ. Devel. Commission
P.O. Box 12728, Capitol Station
Austin, TX   78711
(512) 472-5039

Tex. Foreign Trade Center of
Dallas
P.O. Box 50007
Dallas, TX   75250
(214) 570-1455

Tex. Industrial Devel. Council
Inc.
P.O. Box 1002
College Station, TX   77841
(409) 845-2911

Tex. Intl. Business Assn.
P.O. Box 29334
Dallas, TX   75229
(214) 692-1214

U.S. Chamber of Commerce
4835 LBJ Freeway, Suite 750
Dallas, TX   75324
(214) 387-0404

U.S. Customs Service

P.O. Box 61050
DFW Airport, TX   75261
(214) 574-2170

U.S. Dept. of Commerce (ITA)
1100 Commerce St., Rm. 7A5
Dallas, TX   75242
(214) 767-0542

U.S. Dept. of Commerce (ITA)
515 Rusk Ave., Rm. 2625
Houston, TX   77002
(713) 226-4231

U.S. Small Business Admin.
1100 Commerce St., 3rd Floor
Dallas, TX   75242
(214) 767-0492

World Trade Assn. of Dallas/
Ft. Worth
P.O. Box 29334
Dallas, TX   75229
(214) 760-9105

Utah

Salt Lake Area Chamber
of Commerce
19 E. 2nd S.
Salt Lake City, UT   84111
(801) 364-3631

U.S. Dept. of Commerce (ITA)
U.S. P.O. and Courthouse
Bldg., Rm. 340
350 Main St.
Salt Lake City, UT   84101
(801) 524-5116

U.S. Small Business Admin.
2237 Fed. Bldg.
125 S. State St.
Salt Lake City, UT   84138
(801) 524-6714

(State of) Utah
Intl. Business Devel. Office
6150 State Office Bldg.
Salt Lake City, UT   84114
(801) 533-5325

World Trade Assn. of Utah
2000 Beneficial Life Towers
Salt Lake City, UT   84111
(801) 355-9333

Vermont

(Greater) Burlington Industrial
Corp., Inc.
7 Burlington Sq.
P.O. Box 786
Burlington, VT   05402
(802) 862-5726

U.S. Dept. of Commerce (ITA)
441 Stuart St.
Boston, MA   02116
(617) 223-2312

(State of) Vermont Agency of
Devel. and Community Affairs
Pavilion Office Bldg.
109 State St.
Montpelier, VT   05602

Virginia

Fairfax County Econ. Devel.
Auth.
8330 Old Court House Rd.
Vienna, VA   22180
(703) 790-0600

Intl. Trade Assn. of N. Va.
P.O. Box 2982
Reston, VA   22090
(703) 860-8795

Newport News Export Trading
System
Dept. of Devel.
2400 Washington Ave.
Newport News, VA   23607
(804) 247-8751

Piedmont Foreign Trade Council
P.O. Box 1374
Lynchburg, VA   24505
(804) 782-4231

U.S. Dept. of Commerce (ITA)
8010 Fed. Bldg.
400 N. 8th St.
Richmond, VA   23240
(804) 771-2246

VEXTRAC (Export Trading
Company of Va. Port Auth.)
600 World Trade Center
Norfolk, VA   23510
(804) 623-8000

Va. Chamber of Commerce
611 E. Franklin St.
Richmond, VA   23219
(804) 644-1607

Va. Dept. of Agriculture &
Consumer Affairs
1100 Bank St., Rm. 710
Richmond, VA   23219
(804) 786-3501

Va. Dept. of Econ. Devel.
Washington Ofc. Bldg., 9th Fl.
Richmond, VA   23219
(804) 786-3791

Va. District Export Council
P.O. Box 10190
Richmond, VA   23240
(804) 771-2248

Washington

Econ. Devel. Partnership of
Puget Sound
18000 Pacific Hwy. Suite 400
Seattle, WA 98188
(206) 433-1629

Exprt Assistance
Center of Wash.
312 First Ave. N.
Seattle, WA 98109
(206) 464-7123

Inland Empire World Trade Club
P.O. Box 3727
Spokane, WA 99220
(509) 489-0500

Nat. Marine Fisheries Service
Fisheries Devel. Div.
7600 San Point Way NE., Bin
C15700
Seattle, WA 98115
(206) 526-6117

NW Trade Adjustment Assistance
Center
1900 Seattle Tower
1218 3rd Ave.
Seattle, WA 98101
(206) 622-2730

Seattle Chamber of Commerce
Trade and Transportation Div.
One Union Sq., 12th Floor
Seattle, WA 98101
(206) 447-7263

U.S. Dept. of Commerce (ITA)
1700 Westlake Ave., Suite 706
Seattle, WA 98109
(206) 442-5615

Tri-Cities Chamber of Commerce
P.O. Box 2322
Kennewick, WA 99302
(509) 735-1000

Wash. Council on Intl. Trade
4th and Vine Bldg., Suite 350
Seattle, WA 98121
(206) 621-8485

Wash. Public Ports Assn.
P.O. Box 1518
Olympia, WA 98507
(206) 943-0760

Wash. State Dept. of Commerce
and Econ. Devel.
Intl. Trade & Investment Div.
312 First Ave. N.
Seattle, WA 98109
(206) 464-7149

Wash. State Intl. Trade Fair
999 3rd Ave.
3501 First Interstate Center
Seattle, WA 98104
(206) 682-6900

World Affairs Council
515 Madison Ave., Suite 526
Seattle, WA 98104
(206) 682-6986

World Trade Club of Seattle
1402 3rd Ave., Suite 414
Seattle, WA 98101
(206) 621-0344

World Trade Committee of
Bellevue
110 110th NE., Suite 300
Bellevue, WA 98004
(206) 454-2464

West Virginia

W. Va. District Export Council
P.O. Box 26
Charleston, WV   25321
(304) 343-8874

W. Va. Manufacturers Assn.
405 Capitol St., Suite 414
Charleston, WV   25301
(304) 342-2123

W. Va. Dept. of Commerce
Rotunda 150, State Capitol
Charleston, WV   25305
(304) 348-0400

W. Va. Chamber of Commerce
P.O. Box 2789
Charleston, WV   25330
(304) 342-1115

U.S. Dept. of Commerce (ITA)
3000 Fed. Office Bldg.
500 Quarrier St.
Charleston, WV   25301
(304) 347-5123

Wisconsin

Foreign Trade Zone of Wis. Ltd.
2150 E. College Ave.
Cudahy, WI   53110
(414) 764-2111

Milwaukee Assn. of Commerce

756 N. Milwaukee St.
Milwaukee, WI   53202
(414) 273-3000

(Port of) Milwaukee
500 N. Harbor Dr.
Milwaukee, WI   53202
(414) 278-3511

Small Business Devel. Center
602 State St.
Madison, WI   53703
(608) 263-7766

Wis. Dept. of Devel.
123 W. Washington Ave.
Madison, WI   53707
(608) 266-1767

U.S. Dept. of Commerce (ITA)
517 E. Wisconsin Ave.
Milwaukee, WI   53202
(414) 291-3473

Wyoming

State of Wyoming
Office of Governor
Herschler Bldg., 2nd Floor E.
Cheyenne, WY   82002
(307) 777-7574

U.S. Dept. of Commerce (ITA)
721 19th St., Rm. 116
Denver, CO   80202
(303) 844-2900

Source: U.S. Department of Commerce, <u>Business America</u>, Vol.
8, No. 16 (August 5, 1985) pp. 4-17.

Appendix C
U.S. Foreign Service Offices in Foreign Countries

Afghanistan
Kabul, Wazir Akbar Khan Mina
Tel. 24230-9

Algeria
Algiers, 4 Chemin Cheich Bachir Brahimi
B.P. Box 549 (Alger-Gare)
Tel. 601425/255/186 Telex 52064

Oran, 14 Square de Bamako
Tel. 390972 and 399941 Telex 22310 AMCONRN

Antigua and Barbuda
St. Johns, FPO Miami 34054
Tel. (809) 462-3505/06 Telex 2140 USEMB

Argentina
Buenos Aires, 4300 Colombia, 1425
APO Miami 34034
Tel. 774-7611/8811/9911 Telex 18156 USICA AR

Australia
Canberra, Moonah PI., Canberra, A.C.T. 2600
APO San Fran 96404
Tel. (062) 73-3711 Telex 62104 USAEMB

Melbourne, 24 Albert Rd.
South Melbourne, Victoria 3205
APO San Fran 96405
Tel. (03) 699-2244 Telex 30982 AMERCON

Sydney, 36th Fl., T&G Tower, Hyde Park Square
Park and Elizabeth Sts., Sydney 2000, N.S.W.
APO San Fran 96209
Tel. 264-7044 Telex 74223 FCSSYD

U.S. Export Development Office
4 Cliff St., Milsons Point, Sydney, N.S.W. 2061
Tel. (02) 929-0977 Telex 27619 USIMC

Perth, 246 St. George's Ter., Perth, WA 6000
Tel. (09) 322-4466 Telex 93848 AMCON

Brisbane, 383 Wickham Ter., Brisbane, Queensland 4000
Tel. (07) 229-8955

Austria
Vienna, A-1091, Boltzmanngasse 16
Tel. (222) 31-55-11 Telex 114634

U.S. Export Development Office, A-1080 Vienna
Schmidgasse 14
Tel. (222) 31-55-11 Telex 116103

U.S. Mission to International Organizations in Vienna (UNVIE)
A-1030 Vienna, Kundmanngasse, 21-25
Tel. (222) 31-55-11

Salzburg, A-5020 Salzburg, Giselakai 51
Tel. (662) 28-6-01 Telex 6-33164

Bahamas
Nassau, Mosmar Bldg., Queen St.
P.O. Box N-8197
Tel. (809) 322-1181/1700 Telex 20-138 AMEMB NS138

Bahrain
Manama, Shalkh Isa Rd.
P.O. Box 26431, FPO NY 09526
Tel. 714151 Telex 9398 USATO

Bangladesh
Dhaka, Adamjee Court Bldg. (5th Fl.)
Motijheel Commercial Area
G.P.O. Box 323, Ramna
Tel. 237161-63 and 235093-99 Telex 642319 AEDKA BJ

Barbados
Bridgetown, P.O. Box 302

Box B, FPO Miami 34054
Tel. (809) 426-3574 thru 7 Telex 2259 USEMB BG1 WB

Belgium
Brussels, 27 Boulevard du Regent
B-1000 Brussels
APO NY 09667
Tel. (02) 513-3830 Telex 846-21336

U.S. Mission to the North Atlantic Treaty Organization (USNATO)
Autoroute de Zaventem
B-1110 Brussels
APO NY 09667
Tel. (02) 241-44-00

U.S. Mission to the European Communities (USEC)
40 Blvd. du Regent
B-1000 Brussels
APO NY 09667
Tel. (02) 513-4450 Telex 21336

Antwerp, Rubens Center, Nationalestraat 5
B-2000 Antwerp
APO NY 09667
Tel. (03) 2321800 Telex 31966

Shape (Belgium), B-7010
APO NY 09088
Tel. (065) 445000

Belize
Belize City, Gabourel Lane and Hutson St.
Tel. 02-7161, 62, 63 Telex BH 213

Benin
Cotonou, Rue Caporal Anani Bernard
B.P. 2012
Tel. 30-06-50, 3017-92

Bermuda
Hamilton, Vallis Bldg., Front St.
FPO NY 09560
Tel. (809) 295-1342

Bolivia
La Paz, Banco Popular Del Peru Bldg.
Corner of Calles Mercado and Colon
P.O. Box 425

APO Miami 34032
Tel. 350251, 350120 Telex AMEMB BV 3258

Botswana
Gaborone, P.O. Box 90
Tel. 53982/3/4 Telex 2554 AMEMB BD

Brazil
Brasilia, Avenida das Nocoes, Lote 3
APO Miami 34030
Tel. (061) 223-0120 Telex 061-1091

Rio de Janeiro, Avenida Presidente Wilson, 147
APO Miami 34030
Tel. (021) 292-7117 Telex AMCONSUL 021-21466

Sao Paulo, Rua Padre Joao Manoel, 933
P.O. Box 8063
APO Miami 34030
Tel. (011) 881-6511 Telex 011-22183

U.S. Export Development Office
Edificio Eloy Chaves, Avenida Paulista, 2439, Sao Paulo
APO Miami 34030
Tel. (011) 853-2011/2455/2778 Telex (011) 25274

Porto Alegre, Rua Coronel Genuino, 421 (9th Fl.)
APO Miami 34030
Tel. (0512) 26-4288/4697 Telex 051-2292 CGEU BR

Recife, Rua Goncalves Maia, 163
APO Miami 34030
Tel. (081) 221-1412, 222-6612, 222-6577 Telex 081-1190

Salvador Da Bahia, Avenida Presidente Vargas, 1892 (Ondina)
APO Miami 34030
Tel. (071) 245-6691/92 Telex 071-2780 EEUA

Brunei
Bandar Seri Begawan, P.O. Box 2991
Tel. 29670 Telex BU 2609 AMEMB

Bulgaria
Sofia, 1 A. Stamboliiski Blvd.
APO NY 09213 (SOF)
Tel. 88-48-01 to 05 Telex 22690 BG

Burma
Rangoon, 581 Merchant St.
Tel. 82055, 82181

Burundi
Bujumbura, Chaussee Prince Louise Rwagasore
B.P. 1720
Tel. 34-54

Cameroon
Yaounde, Rue Nachtigal
B.P. 817
Tel. 234014, 230512 Telex 8223KN

Douala, 21 Avenue du General De Gaulle
B.P. 4006
Tel. 425331, 426003 Telex 5233KN

Canada
Ottawa, 100 Wellington St., K1P 5T1
Tel. (613) 238-5335 Telex 0533582

Calgary, Alberta, Rm. 1050, 615 Macleod Trail S.E.
Calgary, Alberta, Canada T2G 4T8
Tel. (403) 266-8962 Telex 03-821332

Halifax, Nova Scotia, Suite 910, Cogswell Tower,
Scotia Sq., Halifax, NS, Canada B3J 3K1
Tel. (902) 429-2480-1 Telex 019-23566

Montreal, Quebec, Suite 1122, South Tower,
Place Desjardins
P.O. Box 65, Montreal H5B 1G1, Canada
Tel. (514) 281-1886 Telex 05-268751

U.S. Mission to the International Civil Aviation
Organization (ICAO)
1000 Sherbrooke, W. Rm. 753 H3A 2R2, Montreal
Tel. (514) 285-8304

Quebec, Quebec, 2 Place Terrasse Dufferin
C.P. 939, G1R 4T9
Tel. (418) 692-2095 Telex 051-2275

Toronto, Ontario, 360 University Ave., M5G 1S4
Tel. (416) 595-1700 Telex 065-24132

Vancouver, British Columbia, 1075 West Georgia St.
21st Floor, V6E 4E9
Tel. (604) 685-4311 Telex 04-55673

Winnipeg, Manitoba, 6 Donald St. R3L 0K7
Tel. (204) 475-3344 Telex 07-55875

Republic of Cape Verde
Praia, Rua Hoji Ya Yenna 81
C.P. 201
Tel. 553 and 761 Telex 68 AMEMB CV

Central African Republic
Bangui, Avenue President Dacko
B.P. 924
Tel. 61-02-00, 05, 10 Telex 5216 RC

Chad
N'Djamena, Ave. Felix Eboue, B.P. 413
Tel. 32-29, 32-69, 35-15 Telex 5203 KD

Chile
Santiago, Codina Bldg., 1343 Agustinas
APO Miami 34033
Tel. 710133/90 and 710326/75 Telex 240062-ICA-CL

China
Beijing, Guang Hua Lu 17
Dept. of State, Washington, D.C. 20520
FPO San Fran 96655
Tel. 52-2033 Telex 27701

Guangzhou, Dong Fang Hotel
Box 100
FPO San Fran 96659
Tel. 69900 (ext. 1000)

Shanghai, 1469 Huai Hai Middle Rd.
Box 200, FPO San Fran 96659
Tel. 379-880

Shenyang, c/o American Embassy, Beijing
FPO San Fran 96655

Colombia
Bogota, Calle 37, 8-40
APO Miami 34038
Tel. 285-1300/1688 Telex 44843

Barranquilla, Calle 77 Carrera 68
Centro Comercial Mayorista
APO Miami 34038
Tel. (95) 45-7088/7560 Telex 33482 AMCO CO

People's Republic of the Congo
Brazzaville, Avenue Amilcar Cabral
B.P. 1015
Box C, APO NY 09662
Tel. 81-20-70, 81-26-24 Telex EMBUSA 6007 KG

Costa Rica
San Jose, Avenida 3 and Calle I
APO Miami 34020
Tel. (506) 33-11-55

Cuba
Havana, Swiss Embassy, Calzada entre L & M
Vedado Seccion
Tel. 320551, 329700

Cyprus
Nicosia, Therissos St. and Dositheos St.
FPO NY 09530
Tel. 65151/5 Telex 4160 AMEMY CY

Czechoslovakia
Prague, Trziste 15-12548 Praha
Amembassy Prague, c/o Amcongen
APO NY 09213 (PRG)
Tel. 53 66 41/8 Telex 121196 AMEMBC

Denmark
Copenhagen, Dag Hammarskjolds Alle 24
2100 Copenhagen O or APO NY 09170
Tel. (01) 42 31 44 Telex 22216

Republic of Djibouti
Djibouti, Villa Plateau de Serpent Blvd.
Marechal Joffre
B.P. 185
Tel. 35-38-49, 35-39-95, 35-29-16/17

Dominican Republic
Santo Domingo, Corner of Calle Cesar Nicolas Penson &
Calle Leopoldo Navarro
APO Miami 34041
Tel. 682-2171 Telex 3460013

Ecuador
Quito, 120 Avenida Patria

APO Miami 34039
Tel. 548-000 Telex 02-2329 USICAQ ED

Guayaquil, 9 de Octubre y Garcia Moreno
APO Miami 34039
Tel. 511-570 Telex 04-3452 USICAG ED

Egypt (Arab Republic of)
Cairo, 5 Sharia Latin America
FPO NY 09527
Tel. 28219, 774666 Telex 93773 AMEMB

Alexandria, 110 Ave. Horreya
FPO NY 09527
Tel. 801911, 25607, 22861, 28458

El Salvador
San Salvador, 25 Avenida Norte No. 1230
APO Miami 34023
Tel. 26-7100, 25-9984

Equatorial Guinea
Malabo, Calle de Los Ministros
P.O. Box 597
Tel. 2607, 2467

Ethiopia
Addis Ababa, Entoto St.
P.O. Box 1014
Tel. 110666/117/129

Fiji
Suva, 31 Loftus St.
P.O. Box 218
Tel. 23031 Telex 2235 AMEMBASY FJ

Finland
Helsinki, Itainen Puistotie 14A
APO NY 09664
Tel. 171931 Telex 121644 USEMB SF

France
Paris, 2 Avenue Gabriel, 75382 Paris Cedex 08
APO NY 09777
Tel. 296-1202, 261-8075 Telex 650-221

U.S. Mission to the Organization for Economic Cooperation and Development (USOECD)
19 Rue de Franqueville, 75016 Paris
Tel. 647-6327

U.S. Mission to the United Nations Educational, Scientific and Cultural Organization (UNESCO)
1 Rue Miollis, 75015 Paris
Tel. 577-1610

Bordeaux, 22 Cours du Marechal Foch, 33080 Bordeaux Cedex
Tel. 56/52-65-95 Telex 540918F

Lyon, 7 Quai General Sarrail
69454 Lyon CEDEX 3
Tel. 824-68-49 Telex USCSUL 380597F

Marseille, No. 9 Rue Armeny 13006
Tel. 54-92-00 Telex 430597

Nice, 1 Rue du Marechai Joffre, 06000 Nice
Tel. (93) 88-89-55 and (93) 88-87-72 Telex 970469F

Strasbourg, 15 Ave. D'Alsace
67082 Strasbourg CEDEX or APO NY 09777
Tel. (88) 35-31-04/05/06 Telex 870907

French Caribbean Department
Martinique, 14 Rue Blenac
B.P. 561, Fort-de-France 97206
Tel. 71.93.01/03 Telex 912670 MR

Gabon
Libreville, Blvd. de la Mer
B.P. 4000
Tel. 762003/4, 761337, 721348 Telex 5250 GO

The Gambia
Banjul, Fajara (East), Pipeline Rd.
P.O. Box 2596, Serrekunda
Tel. 526 and 527

German Democratic Republic
Berlin, 108 Berlin, Neustaedtische Kirchstrasse 4-5
USBER Box E, APO NY 09742
Tel. 2202741 Telex 112479 USEMB DD

Federal Republic of Germany
Bonn, Delchmannsaue, 5300 Bonn 2
APO NY 09080
Tel. (0228) 339-3390 Telex 885-452

U.S. Export Development Office
c/o U.S. Embassy Bonn

Berlin, Clayallee 170, D-1000 Berlin 33 (Dahlem)
APO NY 09742
Tel. (030) 832 40 87
Com. Unit: Tel. (030) 819-7561 Telex 183-701 USBER-D

Dusseldorf, Cecillenallee 5, 4000 Duesseldorf 30
Box 515, APO NY 09712
Tel. (0211) 49 00 81 Telex 8584246

Frankfurt Am Main, Siesmayerstrasse 21
6000 Frankfurt
APO NY 09213
Tel. (0611) 740071 After hours: Tel. (0611) 745004
Telex 412589 USCON-D

Hamburg, Alsterufer 27/28, 2000 Hamburg 36
APO NY 09215
Tel. (040) 44 10 61 Telex 213777
U.S. Agricultural Trade Office:
Grosse Theaterstrasse 42
Tel. (040) 341207 Telex 02163970 ATO D

Munich, Koeniginstrasse 5, 8000 Muenchen 22
APO NY 09108
Tel. (089) 2 30 11 Telex 5-22697 ACGM D

Stuttgart, Urbanstrasse 7, 7000 Stuttgart
APO NY 09154
Tel. (0711) 21 02 21 Telex 07-22945

Bremen, President-Kennedy-Platz, 2800 Bremen 1
Box 89, APO NY 09355
Tel. (0241) 321609 Telex 244901 ACNBD D

Ghana
Accra, Ring Road, East
P.O. Box 194
Tel. 75346

Greece
Athens, 91 Vasilissis Sophias Blvd. or APO NY 09253
Tel. 721-2951 or 721-8401 (Area Code from U.S.: 01130-1)
Telex 21-5548

Regional Trade Development Office
91 Vasilissis Sophias Blvd. (c/o Embassy)

Thessaloniki, 59 Leoforos Nikis, GR-546-22 Thessaloniki
APO NY 09693
Tel. 266-121 Telex 041/2285

Grenada
St. George's, APO Miami 34028
Tel. 2255

Guatemala
Guatemala, 7-01 Avenida de la Reforma, Zone 10
APO Miami 34024
Tel. 31-15-41

Guinea
Conakry, 2d Blvd. and 9th Ave.
B.P. 603
Tel. 415-20 thru 24 Telex 2103 EMBUSA GE

Guinea-Bissau
Bissau, Avenida Domingos Ramos
C.P. 297
Tel. 212816/7

Guyana
Georgetown, 31 Main St.
Tel. 02-54900 Telex 213 AMEMSY GY

Haiti
Port-Au-Prince, Harry Truman Blvd.
Tel. 20200 Telex 0157 EMPAP

The Holy See
Vatican City, Piazza Giovanni XXIII No. 1, Rome
APO NY 09794
Tel. 656-5031

Honduras
Tegucigalpa, Avenido La Paz
APO Miami 34022
Tel. 32-3120 to 29

Hong Kong
Hong Kong, 26 Garden Rd.
Box 30, FPO San Fran 96659
Tel. 239011 Telex 63141 USDOC HX

Hungary
Budapest, V. Szabadsag Ter 12
Am Embassy
APO NY 09213 (BUD)
Tel. 329-375 Telex 18048 224-222
Commercial Devel. Ctr.: Telex 227136 USCDC H

Iceland
Reykjavik, Laufasvegur 21
FPO NY 09571
Tel. 29100

India
New Delhi, Shanti Path, Chanakyapuri 21
Tel. 690351 Telex USCS IN 031-4589 USICA Tel. 46841

Bombay, Lincoln House, 78 Bhulabhai Desai Rd.
Tel. 823611/8 Telex 011-6525 ACON IN

Calcutta, 5/1 Ho Chi Minh Sarani Calcutta 700071
Tel. 44-3611/6 Telex 021-2483

Madras, Mount Rd.-6
Tel. 83041

Indonesia
Jakarta, Medan Merdeka Selatan 5
APO San Fran 96356
Tel. 340001-9 Telex 44218 AMEMB JKT

Medan, Jalan Imam Bonjol 13
APO San Fran 96356
Tel. 322200 Telex 51764

Surabaya, Jalan Raya Dr. Sutomo 33
APO San Fran 96356
Tel. 69287/8 Telex 031-334

Iraq
Baghdad Opp. For. Ministry Club (Masbah Quarter)
P.O. Box 2447 Alwiyah, Baghdad, Iraq
Tel. 719-6138/9 Telex 212287 USINT IK

Ireland
Dublin, 42 Elgin Rd., Ballsbridge
Tel. Dublin 688777 Telex 25240

Israel
Tel Aviv, 71 Hayarkon St.
APO NY 09672
Tel. 03-654338 Telex 33376

Italy
Rome, Via Veneto 119/A, 00187-Rome
APO NY 09794
Tel. (6) 4674 Telex 610450 AMBRMA or 613425 AMBRMB USIS:
Via Boncompagni 2, 00187-Rome
Telex 614437 or 614431 USICAR

U.S. Mission to the United Nations Agencies for
Food and Agriculture (FODAG), Rome

Genoa, Banca d'America e d'Italia Bldg.
Piazza Portello 6
Box G, APO NY 09794
Tel. (10) 282-741 thru 5 Telex 270324 AMCOGE I

Milan, Piazza Repubblica 32, 20124 Milano
c/o U.S. Embassy, Box M, APO NY 09794
Tel. (2) 652-841 thru 5 Commercial Section: Via
Gattamelata 5, 20149 Milano
Tel. 498-2241/2/3

U.S. Information Service: Via Bigli 11/A, 20121 Milano
Tel. 795051 thru 5

U.S. Export Development Office (Milan)
Via Gattamelata 5 (Milan Fairgrounds), 20149 Milano
Tel. 469-6451 thru 4 Telex 330208 USIMC I

Naples, Piazza della Repubblica 80122 Naples
Box 18, FPO NY 09521
Tel. (81) 660966 Telex ICA NAPLES 720442 ICANA

Palermo, Via Baccarini 1, 90143
APO NY 09794 (c/o Am Embassy Rome-P)
Tel. (91) 291532-35 Telex 910313 USACON I

Florence, Lungarmo Amerigo Vespucci 38
APO NY 09019
Tel. (55) 298-276 Telex 570577 AMCOFI I

Trieste, Via Roma 9 (4th Fl.)
APO NY 09293
Tel. (40) 68728/29 Telex 460354 AMCOTS I

Turin, via Pomba 23 (2d Fl.), 10123 Turin
APO NY 09794 (c/o Amembassy Rome)
Tel. (11) 517-4378 or 79 Telex 224102 AMCOTO I

Ivory Coast
Abidjan, 5 Rue Jesse Owens
01 B.P. 1712
Tel. 32-09-79 Telex 3660

African Development Bank/Fund, Ave. Joseph Anoma
01 B.P. 1378 Abidjan 01
Tel. 33-14-34

Jamaica
Kingston, Jamaica Mutual Life Center
2 Oxford Rd., 3d Fl.
Tel. 809-92-94850

Japan
Tokyo, 10-1, Akasaka 1-chome, Minato-ku (107)
APO San Fran 96503
Tel. 583-7141 Telex 2422118

U.S. Export Development Office
7th Fl., World Import Mart, 1-3 Higashi Ikebukuro 3-chome
Toshima-ku, Tokyo 170
Tel. 987-2441 Telex 2722446

Naha, Okinawa, No. 2129, Gusukuma, Urasoe City, Okinawa (901-21)
APO San Fran 96248
Tel. (0988) 77-8142/8627

Osaka-Kobe, APO San Fran 96503
Osaka Office: 9th Fl., Sankel Bldg., 4-9, Umeda
2-chome, Kita-ku, Osaka (530)
Tel. (06) 341-2754/7 Telex 5623023 AMCON J

Kobe Office: 3-1, Kano-cho 6-chome, Chuo-ku, Kobe (650)
Tel. (078) 331-6868, 331-9677/8 Telex 5623023 AMCON J

Fukuoka, 5-26 Ohori 2-chome, Chuo-ku
Fukuoka-810 or Box 10, FPO Seattle 98766
Tel. (092) 751-9331/4 Telex 725679

Sapporo, Kita 1-Jyo Nishi 28-chome,
Chuoku, Sapporo 064
APO San Fran 96503
Tel. (011) 641-1115/7 Telex 935338 AMCONS J

Jerusalem
Jerusalem, 18 Agron Rd.
APO NY 09672
Tel. (02) 234271 (via Israel)
Consular & Cultural Sections: 27 Nablus Rd.
Tel. (02) 234271 (both offices via Israel)

Jordan
Amman, Jebel Amman
P.O. Box 354 or APO NY 09892
Tel. 44371-6 Telex 21510 USEMB JO

Kenya
Nairobi, Moi/Haile Selassie Ave.
P.O. Box 30137
APO NY 09675
Tel. 334141 Telex 22964

Mombasa, Palli House, Nyerere Avenue
P.O. Box 88079
Tel. 315101 Telex 21063 AMCONS

Korea
Seoul, 82 Sejong-Ro
Chongro-ku
APO San Fran 96301
Tel. 722-2601 thru 19 Telex AMEMB 23108
U.S. Agricultural Trade Office: 63, 1-KA,
Eulchi-Ro, Choong-Ku

Pusan, 24 2-Ka, Dacchung Dong, Chung-ku
Tel. 263-3546

U.S. Trade Center, c/o U.S. Embassy

Kuwait
Kuwait, P.O. Box 77 SAFAT
Tel. 424-151 thru 9

Laos
Vientiane, Rue Bartholonie
B.P. 114
Mail to: Box V, APO San Fran 96346
Tel. 2220, 2357, 2384, 3570

Lebanon
Beirut, Avenue de Paris
P.O. Box 110301
Tel. 361-800 and 361-964

Lesotho
Maseru, P.O. Box MS 333, Maseru 100
Tel. 22666/7 and 23892

Liberia
Monrovia, APO New York 09155
111 United Nations Dr.
P.O. Box 98
Tel. 222991 thru 4

Libya
Tripoli, Shari Mohammad Thabit
P.O. Box 289
Tel. 34021/6

Luxembourg
Luxembourg, 22 Blvd. Emmanuel-Servais
2535 Luxembourg
APO NY 09132
Tel. 40123 thru 7

Madagascar
Antananarivo, 14 and 16 Rue Rainitovo, Antsahavola
B.P. 620
Tel. 212-57, 209-56 Telex USA EMB MG 22202 ANTANANARIVO

Malawi
Lilongwe, P.O. Box 30016
Tel. 730-166 Telex 4627

Blantyre, Unit House 4th Fl., Victoria Ave.
P.O. Box 380
Tel. 635721

Malaysia
Kuala Lumpur, A.I.A. Bldg. 376 Jalan Tun Razak
P.O. Box No. 10035, Kuala Lumpur 01-02
Tel. 489011 Telex FCSKL MA 32956

Mali
Bamako, Rue Testard and Rue Mohamed V.
B.P. 34
Tel. 225834, 225663 Telex 448 AMEMB

Malta
Valletta, 2d Fl., Development House
St. Anne St., Floriana, Malta
P.O. Box 535, Valletta
Tel. 623653, 620424, 623216

Mauritania
Nouakchott, B.P. 222
Tel. 52660/3 Telex AMEMB 558 MTN

Mauritius
Port Louis, Rogers Bldg. (4th Fl.)
John Kennedy St.
Tel. 2-3218/9

Mexico
Mexico, D.F., Paseo de la Reforma 305
Mexico 5, D.F.
Tel. (905) 211-0042 Telex 017-73-091 and 017-75-685

U.S. Export Development Office
31 Liverpool, Mexico 6, D.F.
Tel. 591-01-55 Telex 01773471

Ciudad Juarez, 924 Avenue Lopez Mateos
Tel. 34048 Telex 033-840

Guadalajara, Jal.
Progreso 175
Tel. 25-29-98, 25-27-00 Telex 068-2-860

Hermosillo, Son.
Isssteson Bldg. 3d Fl.
Miguel Hidalgo Y Costilla No. 15
Tel. 3-89-22 thru 25 Telex 058-829

Monterrey, N.L., Avenida Constitucion 411 Poniente
Tel. 4306 50/59 Telex 0382853

Tijuana, B.C., Tapachula 96
Tel. 86-1001/5 Telex 056-6836

Matamoros, Tamps.
Ave. Primera No. 232
Tel. 2-52-50/1/2 Telex 035-827

Mazatlan, Sin.
6 Circunvalacion No. 6 (at Venustiana Carranza)
Tel. 1-29-05 Telex 066-883

Merida, Yuc.
Paseo Montejo 453, Apartado Postal 130
Tel. 5-54-09, 5-50-11 Telex 0753885 AMCONME

Nuevo Laredo, Tamps.
Avenida Allende 3330, Col. Jardin
Tel. 4-05-12, 4-06-18 Telex 036-849

Morocco
Rabat, 2 Ave. de Marrakech
P.O. Box 120
APO New York 09284
Tel. 622-65 Telex 31005

Casablanca, 8 Blvd. Moulay Youssef
APO NY 09284 (CAS)
Tel. 22-41-49

Tangier, Chemin des Amoureux
Tel. 359-05 Telex 33025

Mozambique
Maputo, 35 Rua Da Mesquita, 3d Fl.
P.O. Box 783
Tel. 26051/2/3

Nepal
Kathmandu, Pani Pokhari
Tel. 211199, 212718, 211601, 211603/4, 213158

Netherlands
The Hague, Lange Voorhout 102
APO NY 09159
Tel. (070) 62-49-11 Telex (044) 31016

Amsterdam, Museumplein 19
APO NY 09159
Tel. (020) 790321 Telex 044-16176 CGUSA NL

Rotterdam, Baan 50
APO NY 09159
Tel. (010) 117560 Telex 044-22388

Netherlands Antilles
Curacao, St. Anna Blvd. 19
P.O. Box 158, Willemstad, Curacao
Tel. (599 9) 613066, 613350, 613441 Telex 1062 AMCON NA

New Zealand
Wellington, 29 Fitzherbert Ter., Thorndon
Am. Emb., Private Bag, Wellington
FPO San Fran 96690
Tel. 722-068 Telex NZ 3305

Auckland, 4th Fl., Yorkshire General Bldg.
Shortland and O'Connell Sts.
Private Bag, Auckland 1
FPO San Fran 96690
Tel. 32-724 Telex NZ 2938

Nicaragua
Managua, Km. 4-1/2 Carretera Sur.
APO Miami 34021
Tel. 25494, 23061/7

Niger
Niamey, B.P. 11201
Tel. 72-26-61 thru 4, 72-26-70

Nigeria
Lagos, 2 Eleke Crescent
P.O. Box 554
Tel. 610097 Telex 21670 USEMLA NG

Kaduna, 2 Maska Road P.O. Box 170
Tel. (062) 213043/312074/213175

Norway
Oslo, Drammensveien 18, Oslo 2, or
APO NY 09085
Tel. 44-85-50 Telex 18470

Oman
Muscat, P.O. Box 966
Tel. 745-006 or 745-231 ECO/COM
Section: Tel. 703-287, 702-545 Telex 3785 AMEMBMUS ON

U.S. Rep to the Omani/American Joint Commission for
Economic and Technical Cooperation
P.O. Box 6001-Ruwi, Oman
Tel. 703-000

Pakistan
Islamabad, Temporarily located in AID/UN Bldg.
P.O. Box 1048
Tel. 24071 Telex 952-05-864

Karachi, 8 Abdullah Haroon Rd.
Tel. 515081 Telex 82-02-611

Lahore, 50 Zafar All Rd., Gulberg 5
Tel. 870221 thru 5

Peshawar, 11 Hospital Road
Tel. 73361, 73405 Telex 82-5-264

Panama
Panama, Avenida Balboa Y Calle 38
Apartado 6959, R.P. 5
Box E, APO Miami 34002
Tel. Panama 27-1777

Papua New Guinea
Port Moresby, Armit St.
P.O. Box 1492
Tel. 211455/594/654 Telex 70322189

Paraguay
Asuncion, 1776 Mariscal Lopez Ave.
APO Miami 34036
Tel. 201-041

Peru
Lima, Corner Avenidas Inca Garcilaso de la Vega & Espana
APO Miami 34031
P.O. Box 1995, Lima 100
Tel. 286000 Telex 25028PE USCOMATT

Philippines
Manila, 1201 Roxas Blvd.
APO San Fran 96528
Tel. 598-011 Telex 722-27366 AME PH
Com. Off.: 395 Buendia Ave. Extension Makati
Tel. 818-6674 Telex 66887 COSEC PN

Asian Development Bank (Manila)
2330 Roxas Blvd.
P.O. Box 789
Tel. 807251 Telex 7425071

Cebu, 3d Fl., Philippine American Life Insurance Bldg.
Jones Ave.
APO San Fran 96528
Tel. 7-95-10/24 Telex 712-6226 AMCON PU

Poland
Warsaw, Alege Ujazdowskie 29/31
AmEmbassy Warsaw, c/o AmConGen (WAW), APO NY 09213
Tel. 283041-9 Telex 813304 AMEMB PL

U.S. Trade Center (Warsaw), Ulica Wiejska 20
Tel. 21-45-15 Telex 813934 USTDO PL

Krakow, Ulica Stolarska 9, 31043 Krakow
AmConsul Krakow, c/o AmConGen (KRK), APO NY 09213
Tel. 229764, 221400, 226040, 227793 Telex 0325350

Poznan, Ulica Chopina 4
c/o AmConGen (POZ), APO NY 09213
Tel. 595-86/87, 598-74 Telex 041-34-74 USA PL

Portugal
Lisbon, Avenida das Forcas Armadas, 1600 Lisbon
APO NY 09678
Tel. 72-5600 Telex 12528 AMEMB

Oporto, Apartado No. 88, Rua Julio Dinis 826-30
Tel. 6-3094/5/6

Ponta Delgada, Sao Miguel, Azores
Avenida D. Henrique
APO NY 09406
Tel. 22216/7 Telex 82126 AMCNPD P

Qatar
Doha, Fariq Bin Omran
P.O. Box 2399
Tel. 870701/2/3

Romania
Bucharest, Strada Tudor Arghezi 7-9, or
AmConGen (Buch), APO NY 09213 (BUH)
Tel. 12-40-40 Telex 11416

Rwanda
Kigali, Blvd. de la Revolution, B.P. 28
Tel. 5601

Saudi Arabia
Jidda, Palestine Rd., Ruwais
P.O. Box 149 or APO NY 09697
Tel. (02) 667-0080 Telex 405175 USEMB SJ
Com. Off.:   Palestine Rd.

Tel. (02) 667-0040 Telex 401459 AMEMB SJ
U.S. Agric. Trade Off.:
Tel. (02) 661-2408 Telex 404683 USATO

Dhahran, P.O. Box 81, Dhahran Airport or
APO NY 09616
Tel. (03) 8913200 Telex 601925 AMCON SJ

Riyadh, Sulaimaniah District P.O. Box 9041
APO NY 09038
Tel. (01) 464-0012 Telex 201363 USRIAD SJ
USIS: P.O. Box 865

U.S. Rep to the Saudi Arabian U.S. Joint Commission on
Economic Cooperation (USREP/JECOR)
P.O. Box 5927, Riyadh
Tel. 464-0433 Telex 201012 SAMCOP SJ

Senegal
Dakar, B.P. 49, Avenue Jean XXIII
Tel. 21-42-96 Telex 517 AMEMB SG

Seychelles
Victoria, Box 148
APO NY 09030
Tel. 23921/2

Sierra Leone
Freetown, Corner Walpole and Siaka Stevens St.
Tel. 26481 Telex 3210

Singapore
Singapore, 30 Hill St.
Singapore 0617
FPO San Fran 96699
Tel. 338-0251
U.S. Agricultural Trade Office: Liat Towers Bldg., 15th Fl.
Orchard Rd., Singapore 0923
Tel. 7371233 Telex RS25706 TRIWHT

Commercial Services and Library, 111 N. Bridge Rd. #15-05
Peninsula Plaza, Singapore 0617
Tel. 338-9722 Telex RS25079 (SINGTC)

U.S. Export Development Office (Singapore)
111 N. Bridge Rd. #15-01
Peninsula Plaza, Singapore 0617
Tel. 336-3100 Telex RS25079 (SINGTC)

Somalia
Mogadishu, Corso Primo Luglio
Tel. 28011 Telex 789 AMEMB MOG

South Africa
Pretoria, Thibault House, 225 Pretorius St.
Tel. 28-4266 Telex 3-751

Cape Town, Broadway Industries Center,
Heerengracht, Foreshore
Tel. 214-280/7 Telex 557-22387 SA

Durban, Durban Bay House, 29th Fl.
333 Smith St., Durban 4001
Tel. 324-737

Johannesburg, 11th Fl., Kine Center
Commissioner and Kruis Sts., P.O. Box 2155
Tel. (011) 21-1684/7 Telex 8-3780

Spain
Madrid, Serrano 75
APO NY 09285
Tel. 276-3400/3600 Telex 27763

Barcelona, Via Layetana 33
Box 5, APO NY 09285
Tel. 319-9550 Telex 52672

Seville, Paseo de las Delicias No. 7
APO NY 09282
Tel. 23-1885 Telex 72280

Bilbao, Avenida del Ejercito, 11-3d Fl.
Deusto-Bilbao 12
APO NY 09285
Tel. 435-8308/9 Telex 32589

Sri Lanka
Colombo, 44 Galle Rd., Colombo 3
P.O. Box 106
Tel. 21271, 21520, 21532 Telex 0803-21305 AMEMB CE

Sudan
Khartoum, Sharia Ali Abdul Latif
P.O. Box 699, APO NY 09668
Tel. 74700 Telex 22619 AMEM SD

Suriname
Paramaribo, Dr. Sophie Redmondstraat 129
P.O. Box 1821
Tel. 76459, 76507
USIS: Dr. Sophie Redmondstraat 129
Tel. 75051

Swaziland
Mbabane, Central Bank Bldg.
P.O. Box 199, Warner Street
Tel. 22281/2/3/4/5

Sweden
Stockholm, Strandvagen 101
Tel. (08) 63.05.20 Telex 12060 AMEMB S

Goteborg, Sodra Hamngatan 2
Telex 21165 AMCONSUL S

Switzerland
Bern, Jubilaeumstrasse 93, 3005 Bern
Tel. (031) 437011 Telex (845) 32128

Geneva, 11, Route de Pregny, 1292 Chambesy/Geneva
Tel. (022) 990211 Telex 22103 USMIO CH

U.S. Mission to the European Office of the UN and Other
International Organizations (Geneva)
Mission Permanente Des Etats-Unis
Route de Pregny 11, 1292 Chambesy-Geneva, Switzerland
Tel. 99-02-11 Telex 22103 USMIO CH

United States Trade Representative
Botanic Bldg., 1-3 Avenue de la Paix, Geneva
Tel. (022) 320970

Zurich, Zollikerstrasse 141, 8008 Zurich
Tel. (01) 552566 Telex 0045-53893

Syria
Damascus, Abu Rumaneh, Al Mansur St. No. 2
P.O. Box 29
Tel. 333052, 332557, 330416, 332814, 332315 Telex 411919 USDAMA SY

Tanzania
Dar Es Salaam, 36 Laibon Rd.
P.O. Box 9123
Tel. 68894, 67983, 67979, 68033, 67992 Telex 41250 AMEMB DAR

Thailand
Bangkok, 95 Wireless Rd.
APO San Fran 96346
Tel. 252-5040/5171
Comm. Off.:   "R" Fl., Shell Bldg., 140 Wireless Rd.
Tel. 251-9260/2

Chiang Mai, Vidhayanond Rd.
Box C, APO San Fran 96346
Tel. 234566/7

Songkhla, 9 Sadao Rd.
Box S, APO San Fran 96346
Tel. 311-589

Udorn, 35/6 Supakitjanya Rd.
Box UD, APO San Fran 96346
Tel. 221548

Togo
Lome, Rue Pelletier Caventou & Rue Vouban
B.P. 852
Tel. 29-91

Trinidad and Tobago
Port-of-Spain, 15 Queen's Park West
P.O. Box 752
Tel. 62-26371 Telex 22230 AMEB POS

Tunisia
Tunis, 144 Ave. de la Liberte
Tel. 282.566 Telex 13379 AMB TUN

Turkey
Ankara, 110 Ataturk Blvd.
APO NY 09254
Tel. 26 54 70 Telex 43144 USIA TR

Istanbul, 104-108 Mesrutlyet Caddesi, Tepebasl
APO NY 09380
Tel. 1436200/09 Telex 24306 USIC TR

Izmir, 92 Ataturk Caddesi (3d Fl.)
APO NY 09224
Tel. 149426, 131369

Adana, Ataturk Caddesi
APO NY 09289
Tel. 14702/3, 14818

Uganda
Kampala, British High Commission Bldg., Obote Ave.
P.O. Box 7007
Tel. 59791

Union of Soviet Socialist Republics
Moscow, Ulitsa Chaykovskogo 19/21/23, or
APO NY 09862
Tel. (096) 252-24-51 thru 59 Telex 413160 USGSO SU

U.S. Commercial Office (Moscow)
Ulitsa Chaykovskogo 15
Tel. 255-48-48, 255-46-60 Telex 413-205 USCO SU

Leningrad UL, Petra Lavrova St. 15
Box L, APO NY 09664
Tel. (812) 274-8235 Telex 64-121527 AMCONSUL SU

United Arab Emirates
Abu Dhabi, Al-Sudan St.
P.O. Box 4009
Tel. 336691 Telex 23513 AMEMBY EM
Com. Sec: United Bank Bldg., Flat No. 702
Tel. 345545 Telex 22229 AMEMBY EM

Dubai, Dubai International Trade Center
P.O. Box 9343
Tel. 471115 Telex 98346031 BACCUS EM

United Kingdom
London, England, 24/31 Grosvenor Sq., W. 1A 1AE
or Box 40, FPO NY 09510
Tel. (01) 499-9000 Telex 266777
U.S. Agricultural Trade Office: 101 Wigmore St.
Tel. 4990024 Telex 296009 USAGOF

Belfast, Northern Ireland, Queen's House
14 Queen St., BT1 6EQ
Tel. Belfast 228239 Telex 747512

Edinburgh, Scotland, 3 Regent Ter. EH7 5BW
Tel. 031-556-8315 Telex 727303

United States
U.S. Mission to the United Nations (USUN)
799 United Nations Plaza, New York, NY   10017
Tel. (212) 826-4580

U.S. Mission to the Organization of American States (USOAS)
Department of State, Washington, D.C.   20520
Tel. (202) 632-9376

Upper Volta
Ouagadougou, B.P. 35
Tel. 33-25-05 Telex 5290 UV

Uruguay
Montevideo, Calle Lauro Muller 1776
APO Miami 34035
Tel. 40-90-51, 40-91-26

Venezuela
Caracas, Avenida Francisco de Mirando and Avenida Principal
de la Floresta, P.O. Box 62291, Caracas 1060-A or
APO Miami 34037
Tel. 284-7111/6111 Telex 25501 AMEMB VE
U.S. Agricultural Trade Office: Centro Plaza, Torre C, Piso 19
Los Palos Grandes, Caracas
Tel. 283-2599 Telex 29119 USATO VC

Maracaibo, Edificio Sofimara, Piso 3, Calle 77
Con Avenida 13, or APO Miami 34037
Tel. (061) 84-254/5 Telex 62213 USCON VE

Yemen Arab Republic
Sanaa, P.O. Box 1088
Tel. 271950 thru 58 Telex 2797 EMBSAN YE

Yugoslavia
Belgrade, Kneza Milosa 50
Tel. (011) 645-655 Telex 11529 AMEMBA YU
AMCONGEN (BEG) APO NY 09213

Zagreb, Brace Kavurica 2
Tel. (041) 444-800 Telex 21180 YU AMCON:
AMCONGEN (ZGB) APO NY 09213

Zaire
Kinshasa, 310 Avenue des Aviateurs
APO NY 09662
Tel. 25881 thru 6 Telex 21405 US EMB ZR

Lubumbashi, 1029 Blvd. Kamanyola
B.P. 1196
APO NY 09662
Tel. 2324/5

Bukavu, Mobutu Ave., B.P. 3037
APO NY 09662
Tel. 2594

Zambia
Lusaka, P.O. Box 31617
Tel. 214911 Telex AMEMB ZA 41970

Zimbabwe
Harare, 78 Enterprise Rd., Highlands, Salisbury
Tel. 791586/7
Commercial Section: 5th Fl., Century House
36 Baker Ave. West
P.O. Box 3180
Tel. 705-835 Telex 4591 USFCS ZW

Taiwan
American Institute in Taiwan (Taipei Office)
7 Lane 134, Hsin Yi Road, Section 3
Tel. 709-2000 Telex 23890 USTRADE

American Institute in Taiwan (Kaohsiung Office)
88 Wu Fu 3d Road
Tel. 221-2444

Source: U.S. Department of State. Key Officers of Foreign
          Service Posts, May 1984.

Appendix D
Foreign Embassies
in the United States

(Washington D.C. - Telephone Area Code 202)

Afghanistan
Embassy of the Democratic Republic of Afghanistan
Chancery: 2341 Wyoming Ave. NW. 20008
(234-3770, 3771, and 3772)

Algeria
Embassy of the Democratic and Popular Republic of Algeria
Chancery: 2118 Kalorama Rd. NW. 20008
(328-5300)

Antigua and Barbuda
Embassy of Antigua and Barbuda
Chancery: 2000 N St. NW., Suite 601 20036
(296-6310, 11, 12)

Argentina
Embassy of the Argentine Republic
Chancery: 1600 New Hampshire Ave. NW. 20009
(939-6400 to 6403, inclusive)

Australia
Embassy of Australia
Chancery: 1601 Massachusetts Ave. NW. 20036
(797-3000)

Austria
Embassy of Austria

Chancery: 2343 Massachusetts Ave. NW. 20008
(483-4474)

Bahamas
Embassy of The Commonwealth of The Bahamas
Chancery: Suite 865, 600 New Hampshire Ave. NW. 20037
(338-3940)

Bahrain
Embassy of the State of Bahrain
Chancery: 3502 International Dr. NW. 20008
(342-0741, 0742)

Bangladesh
Embassy of the People's Republic of Bangladesh
Chancery: 2201 Wisconsin Ave. NW. 20007
(342-8372 to 8376)

Barbados
Embassy of Barbados
Chancery: 2144 Wyoming Ave. NW. 20008
(939-9200 to 9202)

Belgium
Embassy of Belgium
Chancery: 3330 Garfield St. NW. 20008
(333-6900)

Belize
Embassy of Belize
Chancery: 1575 I St. NW., Suite 695, 20005
(289-1416)

Benin
Embassy of the People's Republic of Benin
Chancery: 2737 Cathedral Ave. NW. 20008
(232-6656)

Bolivia
Embassy of Bolivia
Chancery: 3014 Massachusetts Ave. NW. 20008
(483-4410, 4411, and 4412)

Botswana
Embassy of the Republic of Botswana

Chancery: Suite 404, 4301 Connecticut Ave. NW. 20008
(244-4990, 4991)

Brazil
Brazilian Embassy
Chancery: 3006 Massachusetts Ave. NW. 20008
(745-2700)

Brunei
Embassy of Brunei Darursalem
Chancery: Watergate, Suite 300, 3rd Floor
2600 Virginia Ave. NW. 20032
(342-0150)

Bulgaria
Embassy of the People's Republic of Bulgaria
Chancery: 1621 - 22d St. NW. 20008
(387-7969)

Burma
Embassy of the Socialist Republic of the Union of Burma
Chancery: 2300 S St. NW. 20008
(332-9044, 9045, and 9046)

Burundi
Embassy of the Republic of Burundi
Chancery: Suite 212, 2233 Wisconsin Ave. NW. 20007
(342-2574)

Cameroon
Embassy of the United Republic of Cameroon
Chancery: 2349 Massachusetts Ave. NW. 20008
(265-8790 to 8794)

Canada
Embassy of Canada
Chancery: 1746 Massachusetts Ave. NW. 20036
(785-1400)
Offices of Canadian Forces and Defence Research Attaches
2450 Massachusetts Ave. NW. 20008
(483-5505)
Public Affairs Division and Canadian Government
Office of Tourism:
1771 N St. NW. 20036
(785-1400)

Cape Verde
Embassy of the Republic of Cape Verde
Chancery: 3415 Massachusetts Ave. NW. 20007
(965-6820)

Central African Republic
Embassy of Central African Republic
Chancery: 1618 - 22d St. NW. 20008
(483-7800 and 483-7801)

Chad
Embassy of the Republic of Chad
Chancery: 2002 R St. NW. 20009
(462-4009)

Chile
Embassy of Chile
Chancery: 1732 Massachusetts Ave. NW. 20036
(785-1746)

China
Embassy of the People's Republic of China
Chancery: 2300 Connecticut Ave. NW. 20008
(328-2500, 2501 and 2502)

Colombia
Embassy of Colombia
Chancery: 2118 Leroy Pl. NW. 20008
(387-8338)

Comoros
Embassy of the Federal and Islamic Republic of the Comoros

Congo, People's Republic of
Embassy of the People's Republic of Congo
Chancery: 4891 Colorado Ave. NW. 20011
(726-5500 and 5501)

Costa Rica
Embassy of Costa Rica
Chancery: 2112 S St. NW. 20008
(234-2945, 2946, and 2947)

Cuban Interests Section
2630 and 2639 - 16th St. NW. 20009
(797-8518, 8519, 8520, 8609 and 8610)

Cyprus
Embassy of the Republic of Cyprus
Chancery: 2211 R St. NW. 20008
(462-5772)

Czechoslovakia
Embassy of the Czechoslovak Socialist Republic
Chancery: 3900 Linnean Ave. NW. 20008
(363-6315 and 6316)

Denmark
Royal Danish Embassy
Chancery: 3200 Whitehaven St. NW. 20008
(234-4300)

Djibouti
Embassy of the Republic of Djibouti
Chancery (temp): care of the Permanent Mission of the
Republic of Djibouti to the United Nations
866 United Nations Plaza, Suite 4011
New York, NY   10017
(212) 753-3163

Dominica
Embassy of the Commonwealth of Dominica
Chancery: 1629 K St., Suite 500, NW. 20006
(476-5933)

Dominican Republic
Embassy of the Dominican Republic
Chancery: 1715-22d St. NW. 20008
(332-6280)

Ecuador
Embassy of Ecuador
Chancery: 2535 - 15th St. NW. 20009
(234-7200)

Egypt
Embassy of the Arab Republic of Egypt
Chancery: 2310 Decatur Pl. NW. 20008
(232-5400)

El Salvador
Embassy of El Salvador

Chancery: 2308 California St. NW. 20008
(265-3480, 3481, and 3482)

Equatorial Guinea
Embassy of Equatorial Guinea
Chancery: 801 Second Ave., Suite 1403
New York, NY   10017
(212) 599-1523

Estonia
Legation of Estonia
Office of Consulate General: 9 Rockefeller Plaza
New York, NY   10020
(247-1450)

Ethiopia
Embassy of Ethiopia
Chancery: 2134 Kalorama Rd. NW. 20008
(234-2281 and 2282)

Fiji
Embassy of Fiji
Chancery: 2233 Wisconsin Ave., Suite 240, NW. 20007
(337-8320)

Finland
Embassy of Finland
Chancery: 3216 New Mexico Ave. NW. 20016
(363-2430)

France
Embassy of France
Chancery: 4101 Reservoir Rd., NW. 20007
(944-6000)

Gabon
Embassy of the Gabonese Republic
Chancery: 2034 - 20th St. NW. 20009
(797-1000)

Gambia, The
Embassy of The Gambia
Chancery: 1785 Massachusetts Ave. NW. 20036
(265-3252)

German Democratic Republic
Embassy of the German Democratic Republic
Chancery: 1717 Massachusetts Ave. NW. 20036
(232-3134)

Germany, Federal Republic of
Embassy of the Federal Republic of Germany
Chancery: 4645 Reservoir Rd. NW. 20007
(298-4000)

Ghana
Embassy of Ghana
Chancery: 2460 - 16th St. NW. 20009
(462-0761)

Great Britain
(or United Kingdom of Great Britain and Northern Ireland)
British Embassy
Chancery: 3100 Massachusetts Ave. NW. 20008
(462-1340)

Greece
Embassy of Greece
Chancery: 2221 Massachusetts Ave. NW. 20008
(667-3168, 3169, 3170, 3094, and 3095)

Grenada
Embassy of Grenada
Chancery: 1701 New Hampshire Ave. NW. 20009
(265-2561)

Guatemala
Embassy of Guatemala
Chancery: 2220 R St. NW. 20008
(745-4952, 4953, 4954)

Guinea
Embassy of the Republic of Guinea
Chancery: 2112 Leroy Pl. NW. 20008
(483-9420)

Guinea-Bissau
Embassy of the Republic of Guinea-Bissau
Chancery (temp):   care of the Permanent Mission of
211 E. 43rd St., Suite 604, New York, NY   10017
(212) 661-3977

Guyana
Embassy of Guyana
Chancery: 2490 Tracy Pl. NW. 20008
(265-6900-03)

Haiti
Embassy of Haiti
Chancery: 2311 Massachusetts Ave. NW. 20008
(332-4090, 91, 92)

Holy See - Apostolic Nunciature
3339 Massachusetts Ave. NW. 20008
(333-7121)

Honduras
Embassy of Honduras
Chancery: 4301 Connecticut Ave. NW., Suite 100, 20008
(966-7700, 7701, 7702)

Hungary
Embassy of the Hungarian People's Republic
Chancery: 3910 Shoemaker St. NW. 20008
(362-6730)

Iceland
Embassy of Iceland
Chancery: 2022 Connecticut Ave. NW. 20008
(265-6653, 6654, and 6655)

India
Embassy of India
Chancery: 2107 Massachusetts Ave. NW. 20008
(939-7000)

Indonesia
Embassy of the Republic of Indonesia
Chancery: 2020 Massachusetts Ave. NW. 20036
(293-1745)

Iraq
Embassy of the Republic of Iraq
Chancery: 1801 P St., NW. 20036
(483-7500)

Ireland
Embassy of Ireland
Chancery: 2234 Massachusetts Ave. NW. 20008
(462-3939)

Israel
Embassy of Israel
Chancery: 3514 International Dr. NW. 20008
(364-5500)

Italy
Embassy of Italy
Chancery: 1601 Fuller St. NW. 20009
2700 - 16th St. NW. 20009
(328-5500)

Ivory Coast
Embassy of the Republic of Ivory Coast
Chancery: 2424 Massachusetts Ave. NW. 20008
(483-2400)

Jamaica
Embassy of Jamaica
Chancery: 1850 K St. NW., Suite 355, 20006
(452-0660)

Japan
Embassy of Japan
Chancery: 2520 Massachusetts Ave. NW. 20008
(234-2266)
Chancery Annex: Suite 675
600 New Hampshire Ave. NW. 20037
Information Center: 917 - 19th St. NW. 20006

Jordan
Embassy of the Hashemite Kingdom of Jordan
Chancery: 3504 International Dr. NW. 20008
(966-2664)

Kenya
Embassy of Kenya
Chancery: 2249 R St. NW. 20008
(387-6101)

Kiribati
Embassy of the Republic of Kiribati

Korea
Embassy of Korea
Ambassador's Office: 2370 Massachusetts Ave. NW. 20008
(483-7383)
Chancery: 2320 Massachusetts Ave. NW. 20008
(483-7383)
Chancery Annex: 2400 Wilson Blvd., Arlington, VA   22201
(524-9273)

Kuwait
Embassy of the State of Kuwait
Chancery: 2940 Tilden St. NW. 20008
(966-0702)

Laos
Embassy of the Lao People's Democratic Republic
Chancery: 2222 S St. NW. 20008
(332-6414 and 6417)

Latvia
Legation of Latvia
Chancery: 4325 - 17th St. NW. 20011
(726-8213 and 8214)

Lebanon
Embassy of Lebanon
Chancery: 2560 - 28th St. NW. 20008
(939-6300)

Lesotho
Embassy of the Kingdom of Lesotho
Chancery: Caravel Bldg., Suite 300,
1601 Connecticut Ave. NW. 20009
(462-4190 to 4192)

Liberia
Embassy of the Republic of Liberia
Chancery: 5201 - 16th St. NW. 20011
(723-0437 to 0440)

Lithuania
Legation of Lithuania
Chancery: 2622 - 16th St. NW. 20009
(234-5860)

Luxembourg
Embassy of Luxembourg
Chancery: 2200 Massachusetts Ave. NW. 20008
(265-4171)

Madagascar
Embassy of the Democratic Republic of Madagascar
Chancery: 2374 Massachusetts Ave. NW. 20008
(265-5525 and 5526)

Malawi
Malawi Embassy
Chancery: Bristol House, 1400 - 20th St. NW. 20036
(296-5530)

Malaysia
Embassy of Malaysia
Chancery: 2401 Massachusetts Ave. NW. 20008
Annex: 1900 - 24th St. NW. 20008
(328-2700)

Mali
Embassy of the Republic of Mali
Chancery: 2130 R St. NW. 20008
(332-2249 and 2250)

Malta
Embassy of Malta
Chancery: 2017 Connecticut Ave. NW. 20008
(462-3611 and 3612)

Mauritania
Embassy of the Islamic Republic of Mauritania
Chancery: 2129 Leroy Pl. NW. 20008
(232-5700)

Mauritius
Embassy of Mauritius
Chancery: Suite 134, 4301 Connecticut Ave. NW. 20008
(244-1491 and 1492)

Mexico
Embassy of Mexico
Chancery: 2829 - 16th St. NW. 20009
(234-6000)

Morocco
Embassy of Morocco
Chancery: 1601 - 21st St. NW. 20009
(462-7979 to 7982, inclusive)

Mozambique
Embassy of the People's Republic of Mozambique
Chancery: 1990 Mgt. NW., Suite 570, 20036
(293-7146)

Nauru
Embassy of the Republic of Nauru

Nepal
Royal Nepalese Embassy
Chancery: 2131 Leroy Pl. NW. 20008
(667-4550)

Netherlands
Embassy of the Netherlands
Chancery: 4200 Linnean Ave. NW. 20008
(244-5300; after 6 p.m. 244-5304)

New Zealand
Embassy of New Zealand
Chancery: 37 Observatory Cir. NW. 20008
(328-4800)

Nicaragua
Embassy of Nicaragua
Chancery: 1627 New Hampshire Ave. NW. 20009
(387-4371 and 4372)

Niger
Embassy of the Republic of Niger
Chancery: 2204 R St. NW. 20008
(483-4224 to 4227, inclusive)

Nigeria
Embassy of Nigeria
Chancery: 2201 M St. NW. 20037
(822-1500)

Norway
Royal Norwegian Embassy
Chancery: 2720 - 34th St. NW. 20008
(333-6000)

Oman
Embassy of the Sultanate of Oman
Chancery: 2342 Massachusetts Ave. NW. 20008
(387-1980, 81, 82)

Pakistan
Embassy of Pakistan
Chancery: 2315 Massachusetts Ave. NW. 20008
(939-6200)
Chancery Annex: 2201 R St. NW. 20008
(939-6205)

Panama
Embassy of Panama
Chancery: 2862 McGill Terrace NW. 20008
(483-1407)

Papua New Guinea
Embassy of Papua New Guinea
Chancery: 1140 - 19th St. NW. 20036, Suite 503
(659-0856)

Paraguay
Embassy of Paraguay
Chancery: 2400 Massachusetts Ave. NW. 20008
(483-6960, 61, 62)

Peru
Embassy of Peru
Chancery: 1700 Massachusetts Ave. NW. 20036
(833-9860 to 9869)

Philippines
Embassy of the Philippines
Chancery: 1617 Massachusetts Ave. NW. 20036
(483-1414)

Poland
Embassy of the Polish People's Republic
Chancery: 2640 - 16th St. NW. 20009
(234-3800, 3801, 3802)

Portugal
Embassy of Portugal
Chancery: 2125 Kalorama Rd. NW. 20008
(328-8610)

Qatar
Embasssy of the State of Qatar
Chancery: Suite 1180, 600 New Hampshire Ave. NW. 20037
Chancery Annex: 600 New Hampshire Ave., Suite 610, NW. 20037
(338-0111)

Romania
Embassy of the Socialist Republic of Romania
Chancery: 1607 - 23rd St. NW. 20008
(232-4747)

Rwanda
Embassy of the Republic of Rwanda
Chancery: 1714 New Hampshire Ave. NW. 20009
(232-2882)

Saint Christopher (St. Kitts) and Nevis
Embassy of Saint Christopher (St. Kitts) and Nevis
Chancery: 1730 Rhode Island Ave., Suite 501, NW. 20036
(833-3550)

Saint Lucia
Embassy of Saint Lucia
Chancery: 2100 M St., Suite 309, NW. 20037
(463-7378, 7379)

Saint Vincent and the Grenadines
Embassy of Saint Vincent and the Grenadines

Sao Tome and Principe
Embassy of Sao Tome and Principe
Chancery (temp):   801 Second Ave., Suite 1504
New York, NY   10017
(212) 697-4211

Saudi Arabia
Embassy of Saudi Arabia
Chancery: 601 New Hampshire Ave., NW. 20037
(342-3800)

Senegal
Embassy of the Republic of Senegal
Chancery: 2112 Wyoming Ave. NW. 20008
(234-0540 and 0541)

Seychelles
Embassy of the Republic of Seychelles
Chancery (temp):   care of the Permanent Mission of Seychelles
to the United Nations
820 Second Ave., Suite 203, New York, NY   10017
(212) 687-9766

Sierra Leone
Embassy of Sierra Leone
Chancery: 1701 - 19th St. NW. 20009
(939-9261)

Singapore
Embassy of Singapore
Chancery: 1824 R St. NW. 20009
(667-7555)

Solomon Islands
Embassy of the Solomon Islands

Somalia
Embassy of the Somali Democratic Republic
Chancery: Suite 710, 600 New Hampshire Ave. NW. 20037
(342-1575)

South Africa
Embassy of South Africa
Chancery: 3051 Massachusetts Ave. NW. 20008
(232-4400)
Chancery Annex: 4801 Massachusetts Ave. NW. 20016
(966-1650)

Spain
Embassy of Spain
Chancery: 2700 - 15th St. NW. 20009
(265-0190 and 0191)

Sri Lanka
Embassy of the Democratic Socialist Republic of Sri Lanka

Chancery: 2148 Wyoming Ave. NW. 20008
(483-4025, 4026, 4027, and 4028)

Sudan
Embassy of the Democratic Republic of the Sudan
Chancery: 2210 Massachusetts Ave. NW. 20008
(338-8565 to 8570)

Suriname
Embassy of the Republic of Suriname
Chancery: Suite 711, 2600 Virginia Ave. NW. 20037
(338-6980, 6983, 6985)

Swaziland
Embassy of the Kingdom of Swaziland
Chancery: 4301 Connecticut Ave. NW. 20008
(362-6683)

Sweden
Swedish Embassy
Chancery: Suite 1200, 600 New Hampshire Ave. NW. 20037
(298-3500)

Switzerland
Embassy of Switzerland
Chancery: 2900 Cathedral Ave. NW. 20008
(745-7900)

Syria
Embassy of the Syrian Arab Republic
Chancery: 2215 Wyoming Ave. NW. 20008
(232-6313)

Tanzania
Embassy of the United Republic of Tanzania
Chancery: 2139 R St. NW. 20008
(939-6125)

Thailand
Embassy of Thailand
Chancery: 2300 Kalorama Rd. NW. 20008
(483-7200)

Togo
Embassy of the Republic of Togo

Chancery: 2208 Massachusetts Ave. NW. 20008
(234-4212 and 4213)

Tonga
Embassy of the Kingdom of Tonga

Trinidad and Tobago
Embassy of Trinidad and Tobago
Chancery: 1708 Massachusetts Ave. NW. 20036
(467-6490)

Tunisia
Embassy of Tunisia
Chancery: 2408 Massachusetts Ave. NW. 20008
(234-6644)

Turkey
Embassy of the Republic of Turkey
Chancery: 1606 - 23rd St. NW. 20008
(387-3200)

Tuvalu
Embassy of Tuvalu

Uganda
Embassy of the Republic of Uganda
Chancery: 5909 - 16th St. NW. 20011
(726-7100, 7101, and 7102)

Union of Soviet Socialist Republics
Embassy of the Union of Soviet Socialist Republics
Chancery: 1125 - 16th St. NW. 20036
(628-7551, 628-8548)

United Arab Emirates
Embassy of the United Arab Emirates
Chancery: Suite 740, 600 New Hampshire Ave. NW. 20037
(338-6500)

Upper Volta
(or Burkira Faso)
Embassy of the Republic of Upper Volta
Chancery: 2340 Massachusetts Ave. NW. 20008
(332-5577, 6895)

Uruguay
Embassy of Uruguay
Chancery: 1918 F St. NW. 20006
(331-1313 to 1316, inclusive)

Venezuela
Embassy of Venezuela
Chancery: 2445 Massachusetts Ave. NW. 20008
(797-3800)

Western Samoa
Embassy of Western Samoa
Chancery (temp): care of the Permanent Mission of
Samoa to the United Nations
820 - 2d Ave., New York, NY 10017
(212) 599-6196

Yemen
Embassy of the Yemen Arab Republic
Chancery: Suite 860, 600 New Hampshire Ave. NW. 20037
(965-4760 and 4761)

Yugoslavia
Embassy of the Socialist Federal Republic of Yugoslavia
Chancery: 2410 California St. NW. 20008
(462-6566)

Zaire
Embassy of the Republic of Zaire
Chancery: 1800 New Hampshire Ave. NW. 20009
(234-7690 and 7617)

Zambia
Embassy of the Republic of Zambia
Chancery: 2419 Massachusetts Ave. NW. 20008
(265-9717 to 9721, inclusive)

Zimbabwe
Embassy of Zimbabwe
Chancery: 2852 McGill Ter. NW. 20008
(332-7100)

Delegation of the Commission of the European Communities
Chancery: Suite 707, 2100 M St. NW. 20037
(862-9500)

Source: U.S. Department of State. Diplomatic List. August
        1985.

Appendix E
Guide to the International
Trade Administration (ITA)

(Washington, D.C. - Telephone Area Code 202)

Trade Development, 377-1461

    Aerospace, 377-8228

    Automotive Affairs & Consumer Goods, 377-0823

    Basic Industries, 377-0614

    Capital Goods and International Construction, 377-5026

    Science and Electronics, 377-5225

    Services, 377-5261

    Textiles and Apparel, 377-3737

    Trade Adjustment Assistance, 377-0150

    Trade Information and Analysis, 377-1316

U.S. and Foreign Commercial Service, 377-5777

    Foreign Commercial Operations, 377-8300

    Domestic Operations, 377-4767

International Economic Policy, 377-3022

    Africa, the Near East and South Asia, 377-4925

158   Appendix E: Guide to the ITA

East Asia and the Pacific, 377-5251

Europe, 377-5638

Western Hemisphere, 377-5324

Trade Administration, 377-1455

Export Administration, 377-5491

Export Enforcement, 377-1561

Import Administration, 377-1780

Source: _Business_ _America_, November 25, 1985.

Appendix F
International Marketing Journals

American Export Marketer. Monthly.
Publisher: Newsletter Management Corp.
            10076 Boca Entrada Blvd.
            Boca Raton, FL 33433-5897
            (305) 483-2600

**American Import Export Bulletin or American Import/Export
Management.** Monthly.
Publisher: North American Publishing Co.
            401 N. Broad St.
            Philadelphia, PA 19108
            (215) 238-5300

Business Abroad and Export Trade. Bi-weekly.
Publisher: American Heritage Publishing Co., Inc.
            10 Rockerfeller Plaza
            New York, NY 10020

Business America. Fortnightly.
Publisher: U.S. Department of Commerce
            14th St. between Constitution Ave. and E St., N.W.
            Washington, D.C. 20230
            (202) 377-2000

Export. Bi-monthly.
Publisher: Johnston International Publishing Corp.
            386 Park Avenue, South
            New York, NY 10016

The Exporter. Monthly.
Publisher: Trade Data Reports
            6 W. 37th St.
            New York, NY 10018
            (212) 563-2772

Global Import-Export Digest. Monthly.
Publisher: Global Marketing
            116 W. 32nd St.
            New York, NY 10001

International Trade and Development. Quarterly.
Publisher: DAC International
            2100 M St. N.W. #607
            Washington, D.C. 20037

European Journal of Marketing. Seven/year.
Publisher: MCB University Press Ltd.
            62 Toller Lane
            Bradford, West Yorkside
            B08 9BY England

International Journal of Physical Distribution and Materials Management. Seven/year.
Publisher: MCB University Press Ltd.
            62 Toller Lane
            Bradford, West Yorkside
            B08 9BY England

International Marketing Review. Quarterly.
Publisher: Chriss Furey
            c/o Kil Mistry
            60 Kingly St.
            London W1R 5LH England

International Trade Law and Practice. Quarterly.
Publisher: 120 bd. St. Germain
            75280 Paris Cedex 06
            France

International Trade Perspective. Monthly.
Publisher: 1523 L St. N.W.
            Washington, D.C. 20005

Journal of World Trade Law. Bi-monthly.
Publisher: Vincent Press

10 Hill View Rd.
Twickenham, Middlesex
TW1 1EB England

World Trade and Business Digest.   Monthly.
Publisher: Kassanga International of New York
            213 E. 88th St.
            New York, NY   10028
            (212) 427-7176

Title Index

(Numbers refer to entry numbers of listed publications.)

ABOUT THE COMPILERS

JAMES K. WEEKLY is Professor of International Business and Director of the International Business Institute at the University of Toledo, Ohio. He is the author of numerous articles on international marketing and business, and has contributed extensively to *Baylor Business Studies*, the *Illinois Business Review*, and *Michigan State University Business Topics*.

MARY K. CARY is Assistant Professor of Library Administration and Assistant Director of Library Programs at the University of Toledo, Carlson Library.